Scala Test-Driven Dev

Build robust Scala applications by implementing
the fundamentals of test-driven development in your workflow

Gaurav Sood

BIRMINGHAM - MUMBAI

Scala Test-Driven Development

First published: October 2016

Production reference: 1211016

Published by Packt Publishing Ltd.
Livery Place
35 Livery Street
Birmingham
B3 2PB, UK.

ISBN 978-1-78646-467-5

www.packtpub.com

Credits

Author

Gaurav Sood

Reviewer

Román García

Commissioning Editor

Kunal Parikh

Acquisition Editor

Chaitanya Nair

Content Development Editor

Parshva Sheth

Technical Editor

Prajakta Mhatre

Copy Editors

Charlotte Carneiro

Safis Editing

Project Coordinator

Sheejal Shah

Proofreader

Safis Editing

Indexer

Rekha Nair

Graphics

Kirk D'Penha

Production Coordinator

Aparna Bhagat

About the Author

Gaurav Sood is a Scala and XQuery consultant who consults through his own company Omkaar Technologies Limited. He started playing with computers at a very early age and eventually went onto complete his post-graduate degree in computer sciences.

After working for an Indian software service house for a couple of years, he decided to start his own consultancy business. Since then, his company has provided services to a few Tier 1 Investment banks, the government of the United Kingdom, and publishing houses. He has gained an irrefutable reputation and distinction in the industry. Gaurav has previously worked with HSBC, Deutsche Bank, Reed Elsevier, Lexis Nexis, John Wiley & Sons, HMRC, and Associated News, amongst other smaller names in the industry.

When he is not consulting or writing, Gaurav can be seen making a fuss of his family. He likes spending time with his beautiful wife and two sons. He also loves volunteering for charity fund raising through sponsored runs. Gaurav also runs a small charitable trust in Shimla, India (New Life), which helps provide education to under-privileged children.

Acknowledgments

I would like to start by thanking God for the courage and determination to write this book. There are many people I would like to express my gratitude to, for helping me with this book. These people have seen me through this book, provided support, offered comments, proofread my work, and been a critic when I needed one.

I want to thank my family for being my strength, my parents, Satish and Brij, wife, Khushboo, and two little boys, Johan and Jairus, who have been my strength. They have supported and encouraged me in spite of all the time it took me away from them. It was a lingering and arduous voyage for them. I would also like to thank my in-laws, Hardeep and Kawaljit, along with my siblings and friends for encouraging me to consider writing this book. They have always believed in me.

I would also like to thank Packt Publishing, their extremely helpful editorial staff and technical reviewers for enabling me to publish this book and encouraging me every step of the way. I would also like to thank Artima Inc, for their permission to refer to their work.

Special thanks once again to my lovely wife Khushboo. Without you, this book wouldn't have been possible.

Last but not the least: I beg forgiveness to all those who have been with me over the years and whose names I have failed to mention.

About the Reviewer

Román García has been a self-taught software engineer for the last two decades, and is currently CTO at `Fravega.com`, one of the biggest retail companies in Argentina where he resides. Previously, he worked as a software architect for `Despegar.com`, `ZonaJobs.com`, `DeRemate.com`, and others. An avid cowboy programmer, he is passionate about software development, clean code, test-driven development, and madly in love with the Scala programming language.

I'd like to thank my parents for all their support during the early years, when I found my passion for programming, and, last but not least, to my loving wife, Elisabeth, and my two kids, Manuela and Joaquin, for all the love they brought to my life.

www.PacktPub.com

For support files and downloads related to your book, please visit www.PacktPub.com.

Did you know that Packt offers eBook versions of every book published, with PDF and ePub files available? You can upgrade to the eBook version at www.PacktPub.com and as a print book customer, you are entitled to a discount on the eBook copy. Get in touch with us at service@packtpub.com for more details.

At www.PacktPub.com, you can also read a collection of free technical articles, sign up for a range of free newsletters and receive exclusive discounts and offers on Packt books and eBooks.

https://www.packtpub.com/mapt

Get the most in-demand software skills with Mapt. Mapt gives you full access to all Packt books and video courses, as well as industry-leading tools to help you plan your personal development and advance your career.

Why subscribe?

- Fully searchable across every book published by Packt
- Copy and paste, print, and bookmark content
- On demand and accessible via a web browser

Table of Contents

Preface

Test-Driven Development (TDD) goes hand-in-hand with Agile practices, which is gradually becoming the undisputed standard process or delivering quality software on time. The TDD process originated from the need to better understand and refine the requirements for a system.

Scala has gradually, despite all apprehensions, made a niche for itself as the language of choice for delivering modern versatile systems and microservices. It is slowly and steadily replacing the conventional object-oriented models with more robust and immutable functional constructs. The popularity of Scala emanates from the fact that it provides a bridge for developers to make a transition from the object-oriented to the functional world.

Scala, like all other languages, can allow developers to get so engrossed in its intricacies and magic that the real purpose of the application can easily get lost in over-engineering. Therefore, TDD is required to keep the application code tightly tied to the requirements.

What this book covers

Chapter 1, *Hello, TDD!*, contains a brief introduction of TDD and Agile process. We discussed the benefits of TDD and how and why it needs to be used.

Chapter 2, *First Test-Driven Application*, creates our very first working application using TDD. The purpose of this chapter is to provide a quick win and give a taste of what lies ahead.

Chapter 3, *Clean Code Using ScalaTest*, discusses some of the principles of clean code and delves into the ScalaTest framework.

Chapter 4, *Refactor Mercilessly*, discusses various refactoring techniques and their benefits. The idea is to build a gradual appreciation of the refactoring process.

Chapter 5, *Another Level of Testing*, discusses the concepts of functional testing and behaviour-driven development.

Chapter 6, *Mock Objects and Stubs*, takes an in-depth look into the mocking frameworks that can be used with ScalaTest and Specs2 to enable mocking out the dependencies during testing.

Chapter 7, *Property-Based Testing*, discusses the techniques of writing tests that are driven from inputs provided in the form of tabular data or that is randomly generated.

Chapter 8, *Scala TDD with Specs2*, looks at an alternative testing framework for test-driving Scala code. We also compare ScalaTest and Specs2 so the reader can make an informed choice.

Chapter 9, *Miscellaneous and Emerging Trends in Scala TDD*, explores some new techniques, features, and processes that may soon become incorporated into the mainstream application development process.

What you need for this book

The following software is recommended for use with this book:

- Scala
- SBT
- IntelliJ or Eclipse IDE

Who this book is for

This book is for Scala developers who are looking to write better quality and easily maintainable code. No previous knowledge of TDD/BDD is required.

Conventions

In this book, you will find a number of text styles that distinguish between different kinds of information. Here are some examples of these styles and an explanation of their meaning.

Code words in text, database table names, folder names, filenames, file extensions, pathnames, dummy URLs, user input, and Twitter handles are shown as follows: "The `cancel()` method forces the test to be interrupted."

A block of code is set as follows:

```
test("one plus one with result") {
  val two = 2
  assertResult(two) { 1 + 1 }
}
```

Any command-line input or output is written as follows:

```
$ sbt test
[info] Loading project definition from /helloworld/project
[info] Set current project to Chap1 (in build file:/Packt/ helloworld /)
[info] Compiling 1 Scala source to /Packt/ helloworld
/target/scala/classes...
```

New terms and **important words** are shown in bold. Words that you see on the screen, for example, in menus or dialog boxes, appear in the text like this: "**Tail-call optimization** is where we can escape allocating a new stack frame for a function."

Warnings or important notes appear in a box like this.

Tips and tricks appear like this.

Reader feedback

Feedback from our readers is always welcome. Let us know what you think about this book-what you liked or disliked. Reader feedback is important for us as it helps us develop titles that you will really get the most out of. To send us general feedback, simply e-mail feedback@packtpub.com, and mention the book's title in the subject of your message. If there is a topic that you have expertise in and you are interested in either writing or contributing to a book, see our author guide at www.packtpub.com/authors.

Customer support

Now that you are the proud owner of a Packt book, we have a number of things to help you to get the most from your purchase.

Downloading the example code

You can download the example code files for this book from your account at `http://www.packtpub.com`. If you purchased this book elsewhere, you can visit `http://www.packtpub.com/support` and register to have the files e-mailed directly to you.

You can download the code files by following these steps:

1. Log in or register to our website using your e-mail address and password.
2. Hover the mouse pointer on the **SUPPORT** tab at the top.
3. Click on **Code Downloads & Errata**.
4. Enter the name of the book in the **Search** box.
5. Select the book for which you're looking to download the code files.
6. Choose from the drop-down menu where you purchased this book from.
7. Click on **Code Download**.

Once the file is downloaded, please make sure that you unzip or extract the folder using the latest version of:

- WinRAR / 7-Zip for Windows
- Zipeg / iZip / UnRarX for Mac
- 7-Zip / PeaZip for Linux

The code bundle for the book is also hosted on GitHub at `https://github.com/PacktPublishing/Scala-Test-Driven-Development`. We also have other code bundles from our rich catalog of books and videos available at `https://github.com/PacktPublishing/`. Check them out!

Errata

Although we have taken every care to ensure the accuracy of our content, mistakes do happen. If you find a mistake in one of our books-maybe a mistake in the text or the code-we would be grateful if you could report this to us. By doing so, you can save other readers from frustration and help us improve subsequent versions of this book. If you find any errata, please report them by visiting http://www.packtpub.com/submit-errata, selecting your book, clicking on the **Errata Submission Form** link, and entering the details of your errata. Once your errata are verified, your submission will be accepted and the errata will be uploaded to our website or added to any list of existing errata under the Errata section of that title.

To view the previously submitted errata, go to https://www.packtpub.com/books/content/support and enter the name of the book in the search field. The required information will appear under the **Errata** section.

Piracy

Piracy of copyrighted material on the Internet is an ongoing problem across all media. At Packt, we take the protection of our copyright and licenses very seriously. If you come across any illegal copies of our works in any form on the Internet, please provide us with the location address or website name immediately so that we can pursue a remedy.

Please contact us at copyright@packtpub.com with a link to the suspected pirated material.

We appreciate your help in protecting our authors and our ability to bring you valuable content.

Questions

If you have a problem with any aspect of this book, you can contact us at questions@packtpub.com, and we will do our best to address the problem.

1
Hello, TDD!

Let's begin this chapter with a brief introduction to **Test-Driven Development** (or **TDD**, as it's colloquially known), covering some of its basic concepts. The main goal of this chapter is to give you an appreciation of TDD practices and for you to ascertain what technological niche it fulfills.

This chapter will explore:

- What is TDD?
- What is the need for TDD?
- Changing approach to problem solving
- Iteratively writing failing tests and fixing them
- Significance of baby steps
- Scala
- Brief introduction to Scala and SBT
- Setting up the build environment
- TDD with Scala
- "Hello World" application

What is TDD?

TDD is the practice of writing your tests before writing any application code.

TDD is a practice that is most frequently and strongly advocated by Agile practitioners and theorists. It is one of the major pillars of the Agile methodology. There have been various studies over the years and many white papers published, which clearly state that the use of TDD has resulted in a more successful and robust application code.

TDD consists of the following iterative steps:

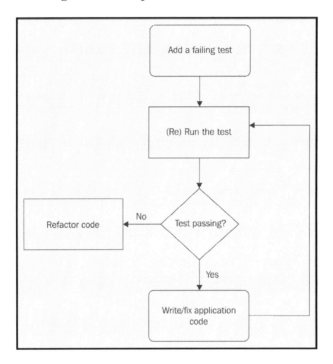

This process is also referred to as **Red-Green-Refactor-Repeat**.

TDD became more prevalent with the use of the Agile software development process, though it can be used as easily with any of the Agile development process's predecessors, such as Waterfall, Iterative, and so on.

At the height of the software revolution in the 1990s, it became evident that the draconian processes and practices developed mostly in the 1980s were slow, officious, likely to fail, and rigid. The Agile development process was created at the Snowbird ski resort in the Wasatch Mountains of Utah. Here, 17 industry thought-leaders met to discuss the problems of the development processes being used with the common goal of creating an adaptive development process that has people at its core rather than requirements. This resulted in the Agile manifesto:

Manifesto for Agile Software Development

We are uncovering better ways of developing
software by doing it and helping others do it.
Through this work we have come to value:

Individuals and interactions over processes and tools
Working software over comprehensive documentation
Customer collaboration over contract negotiation
Responding to change over following a plan

That is, while there is value in the items on
the right, we value the items on the left more.

Though TDD is not specifically mentioned in the Agile manifesto (`http://agilemanifesto.org`), it has become a standard methodology used with Agile. Saying this, you can still use Agile without using TDD.

Why TDD?

The need for TDD arises from the fact that there can be constant changes to the application code. This becomes more of a problem when we are using the Agile development process, as it is inherently an iterative development process.

Here are some of the advantages, which underpin the need for TDD:

- **Code quality**: Tests on TDD make the programmer more confident of their code. Programmers can be sure of syntactic and semantic correctness of their code.
- **Evolving architecture**: A purely test-driven application code gives way to an evolving architecture. This means that we do not have to predefine our architectural boundaries and the design patterns. As the application grows, so does the architecture. This results in an application that is flexible towards future changes.
- **Documenting the code**: These tests also document the requirements and application code. Agile purists normally regard comments inside the code as a "smell". According to them your tests should document your code.
- **Avoiding over engineering**: Tests that are written before the application code define and document the boundaries. Since all the boundaries are predefined in the tests, it is hard to write application code that breaches these boundaries. This, however, assumes that TDD is being followed religiously.
- **Paradigm shift**: When I started with TDD, I noticed that the first question I asked myself after looking at the problem was "How can I solve it?" This, however, is counterproductive. TDD forces the programmer to think about the testability of the solution before its implementation. This would result in solutions, which are testable in nature as we had used tests to derive these solutions. To understand how to test a problem would mean a better understanding of the problem and its edge cases. This in turn can result in the refinement of the requirements or the discovery of some new requirements. Now it has become impossible for me not to think about testability of the problem before the solution. Now the first question I ask myself is; "How can I test it?" This can be done by translating the requirements into tests.
- **Maintainable code**: I have always found it easier to work on an application that has historically been test-driven rather than on one that has not. Why? Only because when I make changes to the existing code, the existing tests make sure that I do not break any existing functionality. This results in highly maintainable code, where many programmers can collaborate simultaneously.
- **Refactoring freely**: Having a good test coverage over the application code allows the programmer to continuously refactor and improve the code while maintaining an idempotent nature of the application code.

Changing our approach to problem solving

Everything we have discussed thus far makes perfect sense in theory, but we need to look at what needs to change in our approach to problem solving if we are to practice the TDD ethos.

I will be more biased towards "me", and will discuss how I made the transition into "TDD land". When I was first asked to build an application using test-driven principles my natural reaction was to doubt every aspect of it. My client at that time had hired a reputable external Agile enablement company to hand-hold developers to learn these new age shenanigans.

My first few questions were "Is it not more time consuming?", "Isn't it QA's job to test?", "Why do we need to test-drive even a very trivial bit of code?", and many more (mostly whiney) questions.

No one gave me a very assuring answer to my doubts, or maybe I was too skeptical to be reassured. So, I pushed myself to endure this and started writing tests first. It was very difficult in the beginning, as I had an obvious solution in my mind and wanted to jump on to writing some application code rather than waste my time with tests. Gradually, it became clearer that the code that was purely test-driven was more robust and had far fewer bugs. Why was that? I realized, when I was doing TDD in its pure form, that I was asking more questions and looking for more failure points for my tests. There were so many assumptions in the requirements that were easy to miss or were deemed too trivial by requirement gatherers. These began showing up when writing tests.

Once you have overcome your initial reluctance and doubts, there comes a stage when TDD becomes a way of thinking. If I am given a problem now, the first thing, which comes to my mind, is its testability.

Let's take a very simple example. Suppose the problem is to write a function to add two numbers. The old me would've bashed a single-line function to return the result of two numbers. No fun in that! Now, I would ask questions like, what is the data type, overflow conditions, exception cases, and many more. Then I would write tests for all these scenarios so they are documented. This is a very trivial example. We will get our hands dirty with another small example by the end of this chapter.

Let's look at what is involved in the process of TDD.

Iteratively writing failing tests

We start with a very minute subset of the problem in hand. In Agile parlance, this problem is also called a **story**. We write a test that will fail for lack of proper application code to make it work. Then we fix only enough of the application code to make the test pass. At this point, we need to restrain ourselves from over engineering and write just enough code to make the test pass. Then we write more failing tests and fix code to fix these tests. This iterative process goes on till all the requirements of the story have been fully met.

At this point, we realize that if our solution is incomplete then this would mean that the acceptance criteria of the story is incomplete. So instead of assuming what should have been, we ask questions to the customer. This leads to better communication between the customer/analyst and programmers. Historically, programmers have worked in a dark dingy room on a set of requirements that they hardly had any input into. Communication between the programmer and the end customer is very important for the success of any project. More often than not, I have seen customers realize the limitations of their ideas once more questions are asked. They also feel more involved in day-to-day progress rather than just getting to see the final product.

Baby steps

Baby steps are the key to a test-driven approach. It is very hard to constrain oneself from jumping to conclusions or solutions just because we think it is best. TDD dictates only to write enough code to fix the test, even though the code seems rather incomplete or trivial. This prevents us from making any major design decisions. When we get closer to the final solution, we will see a natural design pattern evolving. At this point, we can refactor our code. We will discuss this process later in the book.

Brief introduction to Scala and SBT

Let us look at Scala and SBT briefly. This book assumes that the reader is familiar with Scala and therefore will not go into the depth of it.

What is Scala?

Scala is a general purpose programming language. **Scala** is an acronym for **Scalable Language**. This reflects the vision of its creators of making Scala a language that grows with the programmer's experience of it. The fact that Scala and Java objects can be freely mixed makes transition from Java to Scala quite easy.

Scala is also a full-blown functional language. Unlike in other languages, such as Haskell, which is a pure functional language, Scala allows interoperability with Java and support for object-oriented programming. Scala also allows the use of both pure and impure functions. Impure functions have side effects such as mutation, I/O, and exceptions. The purist approach to Scala programming encourages the use of pure functions only.

Scala is a type-safe JVM language that incorporates both object-oriented and functional programming in an extremely concise, logical, and extraordinarily powerful language.

Why Scala?

Here are some advantages of using Scala:

- **A functional solution to a problem is always better**: This is my personal view and is open to contention. The elimination of mutation from application code allows the application to be run in parallel across hosts and cores without any deadlocks.
- **Better concurrency model**: Scala has an Actor model that is better than Java's model of locks on a thread.
- **Concise code**: Scala code is more concise than its more verbose cousin, Java.
- **Type safety/static typing**: Scala does type checking at compile time.
- **Pattern matching**: The case statements in Scala are super powerful.
- **Inheritance**: The mixin traits are great, and they definitely reduce code repetition.
- **Domain-specific language (DSL)**: Scala syntax allows for a programmer to write a natural looking DSL. This ability was carefully built into the original language design. This is a very powerful feature of Scala. Scala test/specs build on top of this feature.

Scala Build Tool

Scala Build Tool (**SBT**) is a build tool that allows the compiling, running, testing, packaging, and deployment of your code. SBT is mostly used with Scala projects, but it can as easily be used for projects in other languages. In this book, we will be using SBT as a build tool for managing our project and running our tests.

SBT is written in Scala and can use many of the features of the Scala language. Build definitions for SBT are also written in Scala. These definitions are both flexible and powerful. SBT also allows the use of plugins and dependency management. If you have used a build tool such as Maven or Gradle in any of your previous incarnations, you will find SBT a breeze.

Why SBT?

The following are the reasons we choose SBT:

- Better dependency management:
    - Ivy-based dependency management
    - Only-update-on-request model
- Can launch REPL in project context
- Continuous command execution
- Scala language support for creating tasks

Resources for learning Scala

Here are a few of the resources for learning Scala:

- http://www.scala-lang.org/
- https://www.coursera.org/course/progfun
- https://www.manning.com/books/functional-programming-in-scala
- http://www.tutorialspoint.com/scala/index.htm

Resources for SBT

Here are a few of the resources for learning SBT:

- http://www.scala-sbt.org/
- https://twitter.github.io/scala_school/sbt.html

Setting up a build environment

We have done enough jibber-jabber to lay the groundwork for getting our hands on the driving plates now. Let's start with setting up the environment so we can write, compile, and run a test-driven application using Scala and SBT.

Steps for downloading and installing Scala

1. Scala can be downloaded from `http://www.scala-lang.org/download`. Download the latest version available.

 Scala can also be installed using Homebrew for Mac by typing `brew install scala`, provided Homebrew is installed. Visit `http://brew.sh/` for more information.

2. After downloading the binaries, unpack the archive. Unpack the archive in a convenient location, such as `/usr/local/share/scala` on Unix or `C:\Program Files\Scala` on Windows. You are, however, free to choose a location.

3. Add the following environment variables:

	Environment variable	Value
Unix/Linux and Mac OS X	SCALA_HOME	`/usr/local/share/scala`
	PATH	`$PATH:$SCALA_HOME/bin`
Windows	SCALA_HOME	`C:\Program Files\Scala`
	PATH	`%PATH%;%SCALA_HOME%\bin`

4. Test the Scala interpreter (aka the REPL) by typing `scala` in the Terminal window.

5. Test the Scala compiler by typing `scalac` in the Terminal window.

 You can test the version of Scala you are using by typing:
`scala -version`
This should give an output similar to this:
`Scala code runner version 2.11.7 -- Copyright 2002-2013, LAMP/EPFL`

Steps for downloading and installing SBT

- On Mac, SBT can be installed using:
  - Homebrew: `brew install sbt`
  - MacPort: `port install sbt`
- On all other platforms, downloading and unpacking the archive can install SBT. After unpacking, add SBT to the `PATH` environment variable. The latest versions are available at `http://www.scala-sbt.org/download.html`.
- SBT can also be installed to run from a JAR. This can be done by downloading the JAR from `https://repo.typesafe.com/typesafe/ivy-releases/org.scala-sbt/sbt-launch/0.13.11/sbt-launch.jar` and then creating a script file to start it. Add the script file to the `PATH` environment variable.

> **Unix**: Download the JAR file. Create an executable script file with this content:
> ```
> #!/bin/bash
> SBT_OPTS="-Xms512M -Xmx1536M -Xss1M -
> XX:+CMSClassUnloadingEnabled -XX:MaxPermSize=256M"
> java $SBT_OPTS -jar `dirname $0`/sbt-launch.jar "$@"
> ```
> **Windows**: Create a batch file with this content:
> ```
> set SCRIPT_DIR=%~dp0
> java -Xms512M -Xmx1536M -Xss1M -
> XX:+CMSClassUnloadingEnabled -XX:MaxPermSize=256M -jar
> "%SCRIPT_DIR%sbt-launch.jar" %*
> ```

This is the barebone setup you need to write in order to create a very trivial project that builds using SBT.

Creating a project directory structure

There is a default project directory structure for SBT projects that defines where SBT will look for application code and tests. By default, SBT uses a similar directory structure to Maven:

```
src/
  main/
    resources/
      <files to include in main jar here>
    scala/
      <main Scala sources>
    java/
      <main Java sources>
  test/
    resources
      <files to include in test jar here>
    scala/
      <test Scala sources>
    java/
      <test Java sources>
```

Build definition files

SBT uses `build.sbt` as a default build definition file. There are other variations of build definition files, such as `.scala` and multi-project files. For the scope of this book, we will only look at the `build.sbt` definition file.

Hello World!

Once we have both Scala and SBT set up, it is time to revisit our understanding of TDD. What better way to summarize than to write a very mundane "Hello World" Scala application using TDD. Let us take this application requirement as a user story.

Story definition
As a user of the application
Given that I have a publically accessible no argument function named `displaySalutation`
When the function is invoked
Then a string with the value `Hello World` is returned.

Notice the language of the story. This is called the **Give-When-Then** notation, which is used to specify the behavior of the system. Dan North and Chris Matte, as part of (**Behavior-Driven Development (BDD)**, developed this language. We will discuss this parlance in more detail when we look at BDD.

Creating a directory structure

Run these commands on the command line to create the directory structure:

1. `mkdir helloworld`
2. `cd helloworld`
3. `mkdir -p src/main/scala`
4. `mkdir -p src/test/scala`
5. `mkdir -p project`

Creating a build definition

Create a file using any editor with the content given underneath and save it as `build.sbt`:

```
name := "HelloWorld"
version := "1.0"

scalaVersion := "2.11.8"

libraryDependencies += "org.scalatest" %% "scalatest" % "2.2.6" %  "test"
```

Use the version of Scala that you got installed locally.

Test first!

How easy would it have been to write just a Scala function that will return `Hello World`? Then again, where is the fun in that? Since we have made a commitment to learn TDD, let's start with the test:

1. Create a `com.packt` package under the `src/test/scala` folder.

2. Write your first test as follows and save it as `HelloTest.scala`:

```scala
package com.packt

import org.scalatest.FunSuite

class HelloTests extends FunSuite {
  test("displaySalutation returns 'Hello World'") {
    assert(Hello.displaySalutation == "Hello World")
  }
}
```

3. Now, on the command line run `sbt test` from under the project root directory `:/Packt/`.

4. You will see a screen output similar to this:

```
$ sbt test
[info] Loading project definition from /helloworld/project
[info] Set current project to Chap1
(in build file:/Packt/ helloworld /)
[info] Compiling 1 Scala source to /Packt/ helloworld
/target/scala/classes...
[info] Compiling 1 Scala source to /Packt/ helloworld
/target/scala/test-classes...
[error] /Packt/ helloworld /src/test/scala/com/packt/
HelloTest.scala:7: not found: value Hello
[error]      assert(Hello.displaySalutation == "Hello World")
[error]             ^
[error] one error found
[error] (test:compileIncremental) Compilation failed
```

Hey presto! An error. Well that's what we had expected. Congratulations! This is your first failing test. Now let's fix the test one step at a time.

Looking at the compilation error, we can see that the compiler could not find the `Hello.scala` class. Let's create a new package `com.packt` under `src/main/scala`. Add a class `Hello.scala` here with this content:

```
package com.packt
object Hello {


}
```

You may be wondering why we are adding an empty class here. This is because we are doing TDD and just doing enough to make the first error go away. Now we will re-run `sbt test` and see output similar to this:

```
[info] Loading project definition from /Packt/HelloWorld/project
[info] Set current project to Chap1 (in build file:/Packt/HelloWorld/)
[info] Compiling 1 Scala source to /Packt/HelloWorld/target/
scala/classes...
[info] Compiling 1 Scala source to /Packt/HelloWorld/target/scala/test-
classes...
[error] /Packt/Chap1/src/test/scala-2.11/com/packt/HelloTest.scala:7:
value displaySalutation is not a member of object com.packt.Hello
[error]      assert(Hello.displaySalutation == "Hello World")
[error]                   ^
[error] one error found
[error] (test:compileIncremental) Compilation failed
```

Again we get an error, but this time it is complaining about a missing member, `displaySalutation`. At this point, we can make changes to the class `Hello` and introduce a member function, `displaySalutation`. It will look like this:

```
package com.packt

object Hello {
  def displaySalutation = ""
}
```

Now re-run `sbt test`. This time the output should look similar to this:

```
$ sbt test
[info] Loading project definition from /Packt/HelloWorld/project
[info] Set current project to Chap1
(in build file:/Packt/ HelloWorld /)
[info] Compiling 1 Scala source to /Packt/ HelloWorld
/target/scala/classes...
[info] HelloTests:
[info] - displaySalutation returns 'Hello World' *** FAILED ***
[info]   "[]" did not equal "[Hello World]" (HelloTest.scala:7)
```

```
[info] Run completed in 227 milliseconds.
[info] Total number of tests run: 1
[info] Suites: completed 1, aborted 0
[info] Tests: succeeded 0, failed 1, canceled 0, ignored 0, pending 0
[info] *** 1 TEST FAILED ***
[error] Failed tests:
[error] com.packt.HelloTests
[error] (test:test) sbt.TestsFailedException: Tests unsuccessful
```

The output is better this time as there are no compilation problems. The build fails because of the failure of the test. Our test makes an assertion that the output of displaySalutation should be Hello World, and our current implementation of Hello.scala (deliberately) returns an empty string. At this point, we can change the empty string to "Hello World" so the content of Hello.scala looks like this:

```
package com.packt
object Hello {
  def displaySalutation = "Hello World"
}
```

Let us re-run the task sbt test. This time we will get the expected output:

```
$ sbt test
[info] Loading project definition from /Packt/HelloWorld/project
[info] Updating {file:/Packt/HelloWorld/project/}helloworld-build...
[info] Resolving org.fusesource.jansi#jansi;1.4 ...
[info] Done updating.
[info] Set current project to HelloWorld
(in build file:/Packt/HelloWorld/)
[info] Updating {file:/Packt/HelloWorld/}helloworld...
[info] Resolving jline#jline;2.12.1 ...
[info] Done updating.
[info] Compiling 1 Scala source to
/Packt/HelloWorld/target/scala/classes...
[info] Compiling 1 Scala source to /Packt/HelloWorld/target/scala/test-
classes...
[info] HelloTests:
[info] - the name is set correctly in constructor
[info] Run completed in 327 milliseconds.
[info] Total number of tests run: 1
[info] Suites: completed 1, aborted 0
[info] Tests: succeeded 1, failed 0, canceled 0, ignored 0, pending 0
[info] All tests passed.
```

This leads us to a solution that is fully test-driven. We can argue about the notion of too much testing and the triviality of the tests, but let's hold off till later chapters. For now, just bask in the glory of having written your first Scala TDD application.

Summary

TDD is a development methodology where application code is driven by tests. In TDD, a failing test is written first and then is followed by application code to fix the test. There is no doubt that TDD works really well in practice, and it complements the Agile development process. This is evident from many success stories and a lot of research done throughout the industry. This chapter had intended to get rid of any reservations the reader may have had about the use of TDD and to give a quick win example. In the next chapter, we will start on a broader problem and will see how the solution can be reached using TDD.

2
First Test-Driven Application

In this chapter, we will cover TDD fundamentals and practices in further detail. We had a brief taster of TDD in the first chapter. This chapter will delve into the more intricate details of TDD. From now on, the book will become more hands on rather than just a textual tome. To keep things simple and to maintain a logical flow, we will be building on the same problem throughout the book. In each chapter, we will add more requirements and make the problem more complicated.

The topics we will explore in this chapter are:

- Testing frameworks
- ScalaTest
- Problem statement
- IDE
- Implementation

Testing frameworks

A testing framework is used for the automated testing of software. It is primarily a collection of postulations, perceptions, and observations which support automated testing of application code. Testing frameworks are not limited to just unit testing, they can very well be used for integration, smoke, and acceptance testing. There are two main frameworks for testing application code written in Scala: ScalaTest and Specs2. Both are equally easy to use and the choice of one over the other will depend on your testing approach. For example, ScalaTest uses the JUnit like testing structure, whereas the Specs2 test by itself is not prosaic but cleaves more closely to an immutability ideal.

ScalaTest is arguably more popular as it makes a transition from JUnit easier. For this reason, we will start with ScalaTest and in later chapters we will compare them both.

ScalaTest

ScalaTest has arguably become the most popular and widely used testing library for writing unit tests when programming in Scala. It is an excellent framework for writing meaningful tests that are not very verbose. The tests are readable. ScalaTest provides the flexibility of being able to write tests in various styles. This makes it a comprehensive framework for both BDD and TDD. We will be discussing BDD in more detail in later chapters.

ScalaTest also integrates very well with various third party frameworks such as JUnit, TestNG, Ant, Maven, SBT, ScalaCheck, JMock, EasyMock, Mockito, ScalaMock, Selenium, and so on. ScalaTest also integrates with IDEs like Eclipse, NetBeans, and IntelliJ.

A quick tutorial

Let's look at ScalaTest in a little more depth with the help of this quick tutorial. All the relevant documentation for ScalaTest is available on the official ScalaTest website: `http://www.scalatest.org`. There are some more third-party tutorials available freely on the Internet.

Adding ScalaTest to the project

The first and foremost thing to start using ScalaTest is to download ScalaTest and the related artifacts as dependencies in your project. As already mentioned, we will be using SBT for build and dependency management.

To add ScalaTest to your project, add the following dependency to your `build.sbt` file:

```
libraryDependencies += "org.scalatest" %% "scalatest" % "2.2.6" % "test"
```

If you are using Maven, use:

```
<dependency>
<groupId>org.scalatest</groupId>
<artifactId>scalatest_2.10</artifactId>
<version>2.2.6</version>
<scope>test</scope>
</dependency>
```

Use the version of ScalaTest that is compatible with your version of Scala.

We covered a very simple ScalaTest example in `Chapter 1`, *Hello, TDD!*. If you skipped that chapter, I would suggest implementing that example before we move forward.

Choose your testing style

A major advantage of using ScalaTest is that it supports a different style of testing. Each style caters to a different set of needs, and it is up to the developer to choose the best style for the type of project. In practice, it is advisable to use the same testing style throughout the project, so there is uniformity in testing and code that can be reused or refactored later.

I sometimes use two different styles in my project, one for unit testing and another for functional testing. This makes it easier to look at the test and know if it can be run in isolation, as is the case with most unit tests. It is recommended to use FlatSpec for unit testing and FeatureSpec for functional or acceptance testing.

Let's look at all the styles briefly.

FunSuite

This is good for the transition from xUnit with vivid test names:

```
import org.scalatest.FunSuite
 class AddSuite extends FunSuite {
  test("3 plus 3 is 6") {
     assert((3 + 3) == 6)
  }
}
```

FlatSpec

The structure of this test is flat—like xUnit, but the test name can be written in specification style:

```scala
import org.scalatest.FlatSpec
class AddSpec extends FlatSpec {
  "Addition of 3 and 3" should "have result 6" in {
    assert((3 + 3) == 0)
  }
}
```

FunSpec

This is more analogous to Ruby's RSpec:

```scala
import org.scalatest.FunSpec
class AddSpec extends FunSpec{
  describe("Addition") {
    describe("of 3 and 3") {
      it("should have result 6") {
        assert((3 + 3) == 6)
      }
    }
  }
}
```

WordSpec

This has a similar structure to Specs2:

```scala
import org.scalatest.WordSpec
class AddSpec extends WordSpec {
  "Addition" when {
    "of 3 and 3" should {
      "have result 6" in {
        assert((3 + 3) == 6)
      }
    }
  }
}
```

FreeSpec

This gives outright freedom on specification text and structure:

```scala
import org.scalatest.FreeSpec
class AddSpec extends FreeSpec {
  "Addition" - {
    "of 3 and 3" - {
      "should have result 6" in {
        assert((3 + 3) == 6)
      }
    }
  }
}
```

Spec

This allows you to define tests as methods:

```scala
import org.scalatest.Spec
class AddSpec extends Spec {
  object `Addition` {
    object `of 3 and 3` {
      def `should give result 6` {
        assert((3 + 3) == 6)
      }
    }
  }
}
```

PropSpec

This is used for writing tests that are driven through a matrix of data:

```scala
import org.scalatest._
import prop._

class AddSpec extends PropSpec with TableDrivenPropertyChecks with Matchers
{
  val examples =
    Table(
    ("a", "b", "result"),
    (3, 3, 6),
    (4, 5, 9)
    )
    property("Addition of two numbers") {
      forAll(examples) {
```

```
        (a, b, result) =>
        (a + b) should be (result)
      }
    }
  }
```

FeatureSpec

This is primarily intended for writing BDD style acceptance tests. This allows for the use of ubiquitous language that can be understood by non-programmers:

```
import org.scalatest._
class Calculator {
  def add(a:Int, b:Int): Int = a + b
}
class CalcSpec extends FeatureSpec with GivenWhenThen {
  info("As a calculator owner")
  info("I want to be able add two numbers")
  info("so I can get a correct result")
  feature("Addition") {
    scenario("User adds two numbers") {
      Given("a calculator")
      val calc = new Calculator
      When("two numbers are added")
      var result = calc.add(3, 3)
      Then("we get correct result")
       assert(result == 6)
    }
  }
}
```

 Most of the book's examples will be built using FlatSpec and FeatureSpec.

Resources for ScalaTest

Further tutorials and documentation on ScalaTest are available here:

- http://www.scalatest.org/
- http://alvinalexander.com/scala/writing-tdd-unit-tests-with-scalatest

Problem statements

The problem statement, which we will define in this chapter, will be used throughout the book. In forthcoming chapters, we will build on this problem statement. We will be looking at building a base conversion API. We will start with an initial base 10 (decimal) number to base 2 (binary) conversions and vice versa. Then, we will add more bases for conversion.

Let's write this down in **gherkin language.** Gherkin is a business readable, domain-specific language that lets you describe a software's behavior without detailing how that behavior is implemented.

Feature: decimal to binary conversion:

As a user, I want to convert a decimal number to a binary number:

Scenario 1:

- Given I have a number A
- When I convert this number to a binary number
- Then, I get a binary equivalent B of the original decimal number

Scenario 2:

- Given I have binary number X
- When I convert this number to a decimal number
- Then, I get a decimal equivalent Y of the original binary number

Scenario 3:

- Given I have decimal number$A$
- When I convert A to binary to get binary number B
- And again convert B to decimal number C
- Then A is equal to C

To read more about gherkin language visit:
`https://github.com/cucumber/cucumber/wiki/Gherkin`

IDE

We will be using IntelliJ IDEA as the IDE for all of the examples and exercises from this point onwards. Eclipse can also be used with equal ease, and if that is your preference, then you can use that.

IDE gives us some advantages over writing out test and application code in a plain text editor, such as code completion, syntax checking, formatting, project management, and a visual representation of the test execution.

 Community edition of IntelliJ IDEA can be freely downloaded from: `https ://www.jetbrains.com/idea/download/`.

After installation, install the Scala plugin for IntelliJ. Navigate to **Configure** | **Plugins**, from the initial IntelliJ IDEA welcome screen, which will take you to the plugins dialog box. Here, you can search for already installed plugins or search for and install new plugins. If you are using IntelliJ version 15 or higher, then the Scala plugin will already be installed. After installation, IntelliJ will ask for a restart:

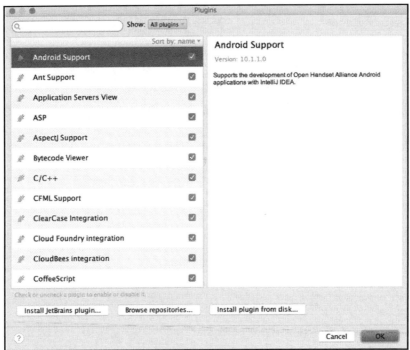

Plugin management screen in IntelliJ

Project structure

We will need to define a project structure similar to the one we did in `Chapter 1`, *Hello, TDD!*. This time though, we have IntelliJ at our side, so we can use IntelliJ to create the structure for us. Follow these steps:

1. From the welcome window for IntelliJ, select **Create New Project**.
2. From the next dialog, select **Scala** from the left-hand margin and **SBT** from the right hand. Click on **Next**:

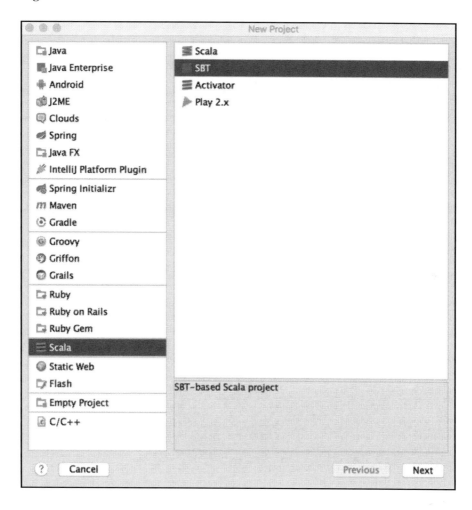

3. In the next dialog box, enter the project and version. This includes the name of project and its location. Name the project `BaseConversionAPI`. It also asks for version information about Scala and SBT you are using. Leave other options as default for now. Click on **Finish**.

This will create a project structure similar to the one we had created in Chapter 1, *Hello, TDD!*. Now add ScalaTest as a dependency in `build.sbt`:

```
libraryDependencies += "org.scalatest" %% "scalatest" % "2.2.6" % "test"
```

IntelliJ will automatically trigger the SBT tasks to bring in the dependencies as soon as `build.sbt` is saved.

Write a failing test – RED

Time to put our programming hats on. We will start with the very first test. It is very important to understand the acceptance criteria before we make a start on the test. Our test will be documenting our understanding of the scenario.

In the normal course of events at this stage, if there are any questions about the scenario, they will need to be cleared up with end user or any representation of the end user.

Let's start with the first test. Create a Scala file `DecimalBinarySpec.scala` for the test under the `com.packt` package inside `src/test/scala` as given here:

```
package com.packt
import org.scalatest.FlatSpec
class DecimalBinarySpec extends FlatSpec{
  "base conversion utility" should "convert a number 99 into a
  binary number 1100011" in {
    var binary:Binary = BaseConversion.decimalToBinary(Decimal("99"))
    assert(binary.number == "1100011")
  }
}
```

While writing this test in your IDE, you will note that IDE will start complaining and/or make suggestions about classes that have not yet been imported. This is one of the benefits of using an IDE, as it does continuous code inspection.

We need to get the test to a state where it can compile successfully though not necessarily run successfully. To get the test to compile successfully, we will create a few more Scala classes that are missing. We will create a `BaseConversion.scala` file with the following content:

```
package com.packt
object BaseConversion {
  def decimalToBinary(x: Decimal) = ???
}
```

And another file `package.scala` with the following content:

```
package com
package object packt {
  trait Number {
    def number:String
  }
  case class Decimal(number:String) extends Number
  case class Binary(number:String) extends Number
}
```

Both these files need to be created under the package `com.packt` inside `src/main/scala`. Just in case you are wondering, the triple question mark in the `BaseConversion` object is not a typo, but instead using three question marks in Scala lets you write a not-yet implemented method, as follows:

```
def finishThisBook = ???
```

This is worthwhile, largely in TDD, as we do not have to think about the implementation at this point. Doing this gets our test to compile.

 There is a funny and interesting post on `www.scala-lang.org`, where Martin Odersky writes, *"If people don't hold me back I'm going to add this to Predef,"* which he later did. The `???` method is defined like this:
```
def ??? : Nothing = throw new NotImplementedError
```

Now, to run the test, you can right-click on the test name and select **Run 'DecimalBinarySpec'**:

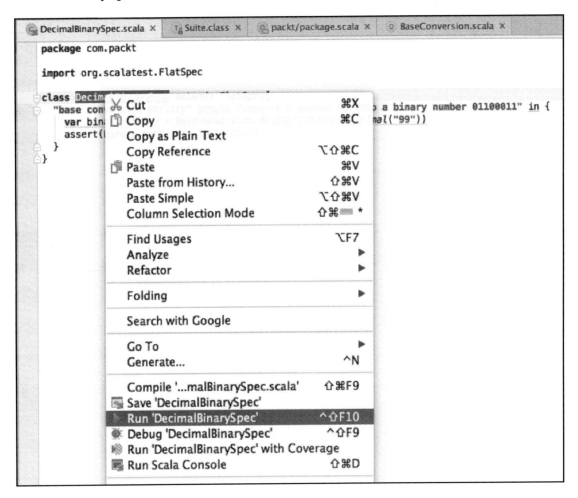

You can see how we are gradually inching forward. It is always difficult to refrain from jumping to the solution. Once the tests are run, we get our first failing test. At this point, the visual illustration of the tests provided by the IDE becomes apparent:

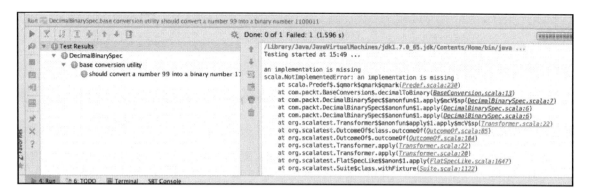

Now, before we jump to fixing our application code to turn the test *green*, we have to make sure that the test we wrote in testing something meaningful and not testing too much. The general rule of thumb is that a test should test only one thing. So it should either have only one assertion, or just the assertions related to a specific functionality. Once we are happy with the test, we will not change the test code anymore so that the premise it is testing is not compromised.

Writing application code to fix the test – GREEN

Now we will write code in our application class to fix the test, that is, for it to go green. This will be done in baby steps, and we will only fix the issue the test complains about in each of the steps. This is where the term "test-driven" takes root. Our test is driving our implementation. At no point are we free to jump to conclusions.

 As you get better with your TDD, it is forgivable to jump a few steps. For appreciation and empathy with TDD, we will follow TDD in its purest form in this chapter.

From the error we got in our last run, that is, **an implementation is missing,** we can see that the test runner is complaining about a missing implementation of the function `decimalToBinary`.

To make our test pass, the simplest thing we can do is make function `decimalToBinary` return the literal expected in the test.

IntelliJ has a keyboard shortcut *Alt + Enter* that gives you a list of intended actions. Try it by clicking on anything that is highlighted as an error in your code and pressing *Alt + Enter*. It will give you an option of inserting this function inside the `BaseConversion` object.

```
def decimalToBinary(x: Decimal) = Binary("1100011")
```

Rerun the test at this point to see it turn green:

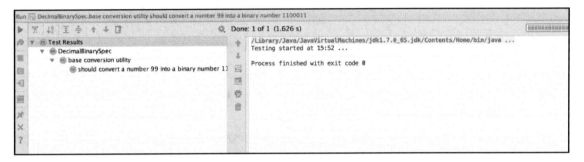

If at some point you want to question the merits and demerits of TDD, this won't be it. We are yet to implement all the other tests to cover the whole feature.

ScalaTest gives us another feature that can help us brainstorm various tests that we should write without actually writing the implementation for them. We will use this to bash out the definition of all the tests we can think of. In my personal opinion, this helps in articulating our understanding at a much broader level, and we know that the tests we are writing are not overlapping in what they are testing. Here is how it changes our test:

```
package com.packt
import org.scalatest.FlatSpec
class DecimalBinarySpec extends FlatSpec{
  "base conversion utility" should "convert a number 99
  into a binary number 1100011" in {
    val binary:Binary = BaseConversion.decimalToBinary(Decimal("99"))
    assert(binary.number == "1100011")
  }
  it should "convert a number 245 into a
  binary number 11110101" in pending
  it should "convert a number 3141 into a
  binary number 110001000101" in pending
}
```

Here we introduced two things `it` and `pending`. Function `it` is specific to FlatSpec and helps with the readability of the test. Using this, you do not have to repeat the initial string `"binary conversion utility"`. Function `pending` is used to mark tests that are yet to be implemented. These tests have the definition of what the test should do but no actual test code inside yet.

You can run the test again to see how it affects the output:

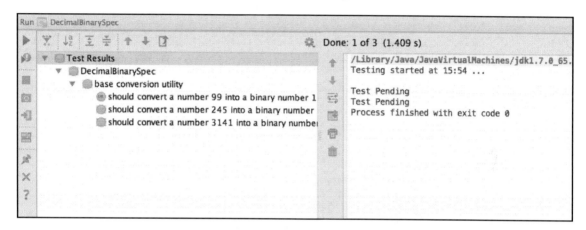

More tests – REPEAT

If you remember form the TDD testing cycle, we had **RED-GREEN-REFACTOR-REPEAT**. We are not at a stage where we can refactor our code, as there is not enough of it yet. So, we skip this step and move to REPEAT, that is, writing more failing tests and then writing application code to fix them. Some of the tests may seem to have overlapping boundaries, but we will leave them be for now.

Let's fill in our pending tests one at a time:

```
it should "convert a number 245 into a binary number 11110101" in
{
  val binary:Binary = BaseConversion.decimalToBinary(Decimal("245"))
  assert(binary.number == "11110101")
}
```

Now we are at a point where we need a more generic conversion algorithm for decimal to binary. So we will start writing our implementation. Decimal to binary conversion is the most mundane one, so you can write your own implementation or copy the one underneath:

```
package com.packt
import scala.annotation.tailrec
object BaseConversion {
  def decimalToBinary(decimal: Decimal) = {
    Binary(toBinary(BigInt(decimal.number), "").toString)
  }
  @tailrec   private def toBinary(num: BigInt, acc: String): String = {
    if (num < 2) num.toString + acc
    else toBinary(num / 2, (num mod 2).toString ++ acc)
  }
}
```

 `@tailrec` will produce a compilation error if a tail-call optimization cannot be performed by the compiler in the annotated method.
Tail-call optimization is where we can escape allocating a new stack frame for a function because the calling function will simply return the value that it gets from the called function:
`https://en.wikipedia.org/wiki/Tail_call`

Let's run our tests again:

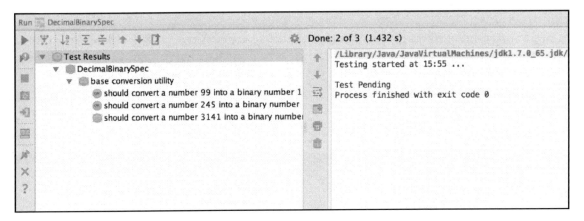

We can see that our solution has worked for both the tests. Now we will implement the third test and if our solution is generic, then the third test should pass automatically:

```
it should "convert a number 3141 into a binary number 110001000101" in
{
  val binary: Binary = BaseConversion.decimalToBinary(Decimal("3141"))
  assert(binary.number == "110001000101")
}
```

Now, if we run the tests again, we can see our solution works for all the three tests:

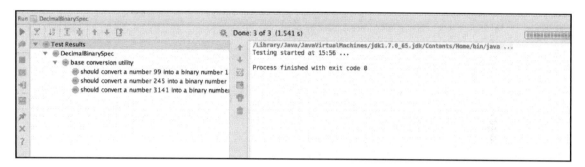

In later chapters, we will be looking into property-based testing using ScalaCheck. This will be very useful in situations like this, by providing a random set of values to test.

In this example, we have seen how to arrive at a solution using TDD principles. To complete our feature, we will be writing `binaryToDecimal` implementation as well. I would recommend that the reader should arrive at the solution for themselves first, before looking at the example here. At all times, make sure you are writing a test first, and the application code is driven by the test in baby steps.

We have not yet made any allowances about our case classes `Binary` and `Decimal`. Right now, it is possible to create a `Binary` or `Decimal` class with the string `"xyz"`. Ideally, these classes should have some kind of check on the creation of the object. This, however, needs to be tested as well. We can't write a functionality that doesn't have a failing test mandating implementation of the functionality.

Our implementation of `BinaryToDecimalSpec` and `BeanSpec` is given here.

BinaryToDecimalSpec:

```
package com.packt

import org.scalatest.FlatSpec
```

```
class BinaryToDecimalSpec extends FlatSpec {
  "base conversion utility" should "convert binary number 100100111101
  to decimal equivalent 2365" in {
    var decimal:Decimal =
    BaseConversion.binaryToDecimal(Binary("100100111101"))
    assert(decimal.number == "2365")
  }

  it should "convert binary number 11110001111110111 to decimal equivalent
  123895" in {
    var decimal:Decimal =
    BaseConversion.binaryToDecimal(Binary("11110001111110111"))
    assert(decimal.number == "123895")
  }

  it should "convert binary number 100000000000001110000001
  to decimal equivalent 8389505" in {
    var decimal:Decimal =
    BaseConversion.binaryToDecimal(Binary("100000000000001110000001"))
    assert(decimal.number == "8389505")
  }
}
```

BeanSpec:

```
package com.packt
import org.scalatest.FlatSpec
class BeanSpec extends FlatSpec {
  "Decimal" should "throw error when initalised with
  a non numeric string" in {
    try {
      Decimal("XYZ")
    }
    catch {
      case e:IllegalArgumentException =>
      assert(e.getMessage == "requirement
      failed: Unable to convert string to number")
      case _ =>fail
    }
  }
  "Binary" should "throw error when initalised with a
  non numeric string" in {
    intercept[IllegalArgumentException] {
      Binary("XYZ")
    }
  }
}
```

Intercepting exceptions

Sometimes, we need to test if the code is throwing an expected exception. This can be tested in JUnit style as used in the test for `Decimal`, for example:

```
try {
  Decimal("XYZ")
}
catch {
  case e:IllegalArgumentException =>
  assert(e.getMessage == "requirement failed:
  Unable to convert string to number")
  case _ =>fail
}
```

Alternatively, it can be tested using `intercept`, for example:

```
intercept[IllegalArgumentException] {
  Binary("XYZ")
```

Both `intercept` and `try...catch` have their own advantages as evident from our implementation. `try...catch` allows access to the exception object for inspection, whereas `intercept` is more succinct.

All the tests in `BeanSpec` and `BinaryToDecimalSpec` will fail, and then we will fix these one at a time. Here is our final implementation of `BaseConversion.scala` and `package.scala.packt` package object.

BaseConversion:

```
package com.packt

import scala.annotation.tailrec

object BaseConversion {

  def binaryToDecimal(binary: Binary): Decimal = {
    val seq = binary.number.reverse.zipWithIndex.map {
      case (a, i) => a.toString.toInt * math.pow(2, i)
    }
    Decimal(seq.sum.toInt.toString)
  }

  def decimalToBinary(decimal: Decimal) = {
    Binary(toBinary(BigInt(decimal.number), "").toString)
  }
```

```
    @tailrec
    private def toBinary(num: BigInt, acc: String): String = {
      if (num < 2) (num.toString + acc)
      else toBinary(num / 2, (num mod 2).toString ++ acc)
    }
}
```

package.scala.packt:

```
package com
package object packt {
  trait Number {
    def number:String
    require(number forall Character.isDigit,
    "Unable to convert string to number")
  }
  case class Decimal(number:String) extends Number
  case class Binary(number:String) extends Number
}
```

Summary

This chapter was intended to be more hands on. We looked at ScalaTest and how it fits in with other unit testing frameworks for Scala. We also looked at different styles and specs, which ScalaTest provides. Most of the examples and illustrations in this book will be using ScalaTest, so it would be worthwhile to do some more reading on ScalaTest. We also laid the foundation for the problem that we will be looking at throughout the book. We will be adding more complexities to the same problem. We will be looking to create a robust test harness by refactoring our tests at every stage.

3

Clean Code Using ScalaTest

In this chapter, we will look at some examples of writing clean test code. You will also continue your learning of ScalaTest. We will explore the following:

- Assertions
- Matchers
- Base test classes
- Test fixtures

 Some of the text and examples in this chapter has been cited with the consent from official ScalaTest documentation at www.scalatest.org. This text and example is copyright of Artima, Inc.

Assertions

There are three default assertions that come out of the box with ScalaTest:

- assert:

    We used this in Chapter 2, *First Test-Driven Application*. This is used for general assertions:

```
test("one plus one") {
    assert(1 + 1 == two)
    assert(1 + 1 != three)
  }
```

- `assertResult`:

This is used to differentiate between the expected value and the actual:

```
test("one plus one with result") {
    val two = 2
    assertResult(two) { 1 + 1 }
}
```

- `intercept`:

We have seen the use of intercept in `Chapter 2`, *First Test-Driven Application*. This is useful in cases when we want to test if a method throws an expected exception:

```
intercept[IllegalArgumentException] {
  someMethod()
}
```

The equivalent JUnit 3 like implementation would be:

```
try {
    someMethod()
    fail("Shouldn't be here")
}
catch {
    case _:IllegalArgumentException => //Expected so continue
    case _ => fail("Unexpected exception thrown")
}
```

In both these cases, if `someMethod` completes normally or throws an exception other than `IllegalArgumentException`, then the intercept will fail with `TestFailedException`. `intercept` returns the caught exception, so it can be inspected further if required, for example, for the message encapsulated inside the exception.

Deliberately failing tests

If you want to deliberately fail the test under certain circumstances then use either of the following:

```
fail()
fail("Failure message")
```

This will throw `TestFailException` with the message, if any, as the errorMessage encapsulated within the exception object.

Assumptions

Apart from the default assertions, we can use the features within the Assertion trait. This trait provides methods that can cancel a test if some assumptions are not met. Note that the test is cancelled but not failed. This can be used to test for some preconditions that must exist for the test to work. For example, the test may be reliant on a database being available. Therefore, before the actual assertion, we can use the `assume` method from the Assertion trait to check for the availability of the database:

```
assume(database.isAvailable())
```

Assertion trait has an overloaded variation of the `assume` method with a similar signature to the overloaded variations of the `assert` method:

```
assume(database.isAvailable(), "Duh!!")
assume(database.isAvailable())
```

Canceling tests

The `cancel()` method forces the test to be interrupted with `TestCancelledException`. It is similar to `fail()`, but for the exception. The `fail()` method throws a `TestFailedException`. `cancel()` has the same number of overloaded variations as the `fail()` method with either of the signatures:

```
cancel()
cancel("I cancelled it deliberately")
```

Failure messages and clues

We can provide default information about a method using the clue. The clue message forms part of the detailed message inside the exception. Both `assert` and `assertResult` provide a way to give this extra information, whereas `intercept` does not. `intercept` can be wrapped with a `withClue` method to provide this extra information using either of the following:

```
assert("Hello".length == 5, "Message")

assertResult(5, "Message") {"Hello".length}

withClue("Message") {
    intercept[IllegalArgumentException] {
        someMethod()
```

```
    }
  }
```

In all these three implementations, extra information `"Message"` is added to the detailed message of the exception thrown. The `withClue` method will only modify the detailed message of an exception that is mixin the `ModifiableMessage` trait.

Matchers

Along with assertion, ScalaTest also supports a **domain-specific language (DSL)** for expressing assertions in the test. This is achieved using the word `should`. This is done by mixing in Matchers:

```
import org.scalatest._
class PacktSpec extends FlatSpec with Matchers
```

Alternatively, members of the trait can be imported explicitly:

```
import Matchers._
```

ScalaTest has the Matchers trait, which you can mixin to your `suite` class to write equality assertions like this:

```
message should equal ("Hello World")
```

`message` is a variable and can be of any type. In all the preceding cases, if the equality is not held true, then `TestFailedException` is thrown. A detail message encapsulated in this exception will explain the problem and why the test failed.

Alternatively, you can mixin `MustMatchers` as an alternative to Matchers, which proves same syntax and meaning as the Matchers trait, but uses the verb `must` instead of `should`.

Matchers for equality

ScalaTest Matchers provide five different ways to check for equality:

```
message should be ("Hello World")
message shouldBe "Hello World"
message should equal ("Hello World")
message should === ("Hello to World")
message shouldEqual "Hello World"
```

Matchers for instance and identity checks of objects

To check if an object is an instance of a class, you can use be a or be an:

```
message shouldBe a [String]
person should not be an [Animal]
```

Any type parameters will be erased on JVM, therefore, it's recommended to use underscore for type:

```
names should be a [Seq[_]]
```

To check if two references to an object refer to same object we can use:

```
obj1 should be theSameInstanceAs obj2
```

Matchers for size and length

Both size and length can be checked using the following syntax:

```
message should have length 10
population should have size 200
```

The length parameter can be used for any type T for which an implicit Length[T] is available in scope. Similarly, size can be used for any type T for which an implicit Size[T] is available in scope. The length parameter can also be used.

Matching strings

There are tests for the usual starting, ending, and inclusion of a string:

```
message should startWith ("Hello")
message should endWith ("rld")
message should not include ("Batman")
```

Here, the string to match with can be replaced with a regular expression:

```
message should endWith ("wor.d")
```

We can also test a full match of the string with a regular expression:

```
message should fullyMatch regex ("[A-Za-zs]+")
```

The `regex` parameter can also be combined with a requirement for groups matching, for example:

```
"123zyx321" should startWith regex ("([d]+)" withGroups ("123"))
```

Matching greater and less than

Any type which has an implicit `Ordering[T]` available can be a candidate for greater than, less than, greater than or equal, and less than or equal:

```
number should be < 7
number should be <= 7
number should be >= 7
number should be > 7
```

Matching Boolean properties

A method that returns a Boolean can be tested by prepending a symbol (`'`) to the method name, for example:

```
war shouldBe 'over
```

Here, `over` is a method returning a Boolean.

In case `over` does not return true, then ScalaTest will return `TestFailedException` with this detailed message:

war should be over

Optionally, we can use `a` or `an` if we think it will improve readability of the test:

```
earth should be a 'planet
```

If this fails, then the message would be:

earth should be a planet

Matching number within ranges

Sometimes, we would want to test if the number is within a certain range of an expected value. This can be tested using the +– operator, for example:

```
voltage should equal (12.0 +- 0.5)
voltage should be (12.0 +- 0.5)
voltage shouldBe 240 +- 10
```

Matching emptiness

We can test if an object is empty using the `empty` Matcher. The list of names should not be empty here. The `empty` Matcher can be used with any type T which has an implicit `Emptiness[T]`:

```
None shouldBe empty
Some(1) should not be empty
"" shouldBe empty
new java.util.HashMap[Int, Int] shouldBe empty
new { def isEmpty = true} shouldBe empty
Array(1, 2, 3) should not be empty
```

Writing your own BeMatchers

You can create a custom `BeMatcher`. For example, you can write a lowercase Matcher that can test if a string is in lowercase:

```
message shouldBe lowercase
```

Some more Matchers

We covered the most basic of the Matchers in the previous section. Further on, we have some more Matchers that are not as generic as the basic Matchers from last section.

Matchers for containers

We can test if a container has a particular element:

```
listOfNames should contain("Bob")
```

This can be used with any type T that has an implicit type
`org.scalatest.enabler.Containing[T]`. In the Containing companion object,
implicits are provided for types `GenTraversable[E]`, `java.util.Collection[E]`,
`java.util.Map[K, V]`, `String`, `Array[E]`, and `Option[E]`.

```
(List("Hi", "Di", "Ho") should contain ("ho")) (after being lowerCased)
```

Note that when you use the explicitly DSL with contain, you need to wrap the entire
contain expression in parentheses.

The other DSLs we can use with contain is `one of`, `atLeastOneOf`, and `noneOf`. Here are
some examples:

```
List(1, 2, 3, 4, 5) should contain oneOf (5, 7, 9)
List(1, 2, 3, 4, 5) should contain noneOf (7, 8, 9)
Some(0) should contain noneOf (7, 8, 9)
(Array("Doe", "Ray", "Me") should contain oneOf ("X", "RAY", "BEAM"))
(after being lowerCased)
```

There are some Matchers DSL that are used in particular to test containment in sequences.

Here are some examples:

```
List(1, 2, 2, 3, 3, 3) should contain inOrderOnly (1, 2, 3)
List(0, 1, 2, 2, 99, 3, 3, 3, 5) should contain inOrder (1, 2, 3)
List(1, 2, 3) should contain theSameElementsInOrderAs
collection.mutable.TreeSet(3, 2, 1)
```

You can also ask whether the elements of *sortable* objects (such as arrays, Java Lists, and
GenSeqs) are in sorted order, as follows:

```
List(1, 2, 3) shouldBe sorted
```

There are some very useful inspector shorthands that can be used to make determinations on sequences. For example, a code such as this:

```
val xs = List(1, 2, 3)
forAll (xs) { x => x should be < 10 }
```

It can be written as:

```
all (xs) should be < 10
```

Here is a full list of inspectors:

- `all`: This succeeds if the assertion holds true for every element
- `atLeast`: This succeeds if the assertion holds true for at least the specified number of elements
- `atMost`: This succeeds if the assertion holds true for at most the specified number of elements
- `between`: This succeeds if the assertion holds true for the specified number of elements between minimum and maximum number of elements, inclusivly
- `every`: This is same as `all`, but lists all failing elements if it fails (whereas `all` just reports the first failing element)
- `exactly`: This succeeds if the assertion holds true for exactly the specified number of elements

Here are their examples:

```
all (xs) should be > 0
atMost(2, xs) should be >= 4
atLeast(3, xs) should be < 5
between(2, 3, xs) should (be > 1 and be < 5)
exactly (2, xs) should be <= 2
every (xs) should be < 10
```

Combining Matchers with logical expressions

It is possible to combine multiple Matcher expressions with and and/or not, but the expressions need to be enclosed in parentheses:

```
map should (contain key ("two") and not contain value (7))
traversable should (contain (7) or (contain (8) and have size (9)))
map should (not be (null) and contain key ("ouch"))
```

Matching options

You can work with options using ScalaTest's equality, empty, defined, and contain syntax. For example, if you wish to check whether an option is None, you can write any of these:

```
option shouldEqual None
option shouldBe None
option should === (None)
option shouldBe empty
```

If you wish to check an option is defined and holds a specific value, you can write any of these:

```
option shouldEqual Some("hi")
option shouldBe defined
```

Matching properties

Using have, you can check properties of any type where a property is an attribute of any object that can be retrieved either by a public field, method, JavaBean-style get, or is a method, as follows:

```
book should have (
  'title ("Programming in Scala"),
  'author (List("Odersky", "Spoon", "Venners")),
  'pubYear (2008)
)
```

There is a lot more you can do with Matchers. ScalaTest gives you the ability to write your own Matchers. For example, if we need to write a Matcher which can test the file extension, say endsWithExtension.

Here is an example of this custom Matcher:

```
import org.scalatest._
import matchers._

trait CustomMatchers {

  class FileEndsWithExtensionMatcher(expectedExtension: String)
  extends Matcher[java.io.File] {

    def apply(left: java.io.File) = {
      val name = left.getName
      MatchResult(
```

```
            name.endsWith(expectedExtension),
            s"""File $name did not end with extension "$expectedExtension"""",
            s"""File $name ended with extension "$expectedExtension""""
        )
      }
    }

    def endWithExtension(expectedExtension: String) = new
    FileEndsWithExtensionMatcher(expectedExtension)
}

// Make them easy to import with:
// import CustomMatchers._
object CustomMatchers extends CustomMatchers
```

This custom Matcher can be used by importing `CustomMatchers._`, for example:

```
file should not endWithExtension "txt"
```

Dynamic Matchers can also be created like this:

```
val hidden = 'hidden
```

Then, we can use this Matcher as shown here:

```
new File("file.txt") shouldBe hidden
```

Checking that a snippet of code does not compile

Often, when creating libraries, you may wish to ensure that certain arrangements of code that represent potential "user errors" do not compile so that your library is more error resistant. ScalaTest Matchers trait includes the following syntax for that purpose:

```
"val a: String = 1" shouldNot compile
```

If you want to ensure that a snippet of code does not compile because of a type error (as opposed to a syntax error), use the following:

```
"val a: String = 1" shouldNot typeCheck
```

Note that the `shouldNot typeCheck` syntax will only succeed if the given snippet of code does not compile because of a type error. A syntax error will still result on a thrown `TestFailedException`.

If you want to state that a snippet of code does compile, you can make that more obvious with:

```
"val a: Int = 1" should compile
```

Although the previous three constructs are implemented with macros that determine at compile time whether the snippet of code represented by the string does or does not compile, errors are reported as test failures at runtime.

Base test classes

ScalaTest consists of lots of lightweight traits that are focused around solutions for similar or unique problems. This allows us to mix them together to solve the problem in hand.

Testing convention dictates that instead of mixing the same traits in all tests, we create a base class, which mixes all the required traits used by all the tests in the application. This gives a uniform DSL across all tests in the project. There may be cases when one particular tests need to mix a few more traits, and it's fine to do so for those individual tests.

We will be using the same principle in our example application that we wrote in previous chapters. We will create a base class that we will endeavor to reuse for all the tests. At this point, we need to make sure that we are happy to use the same DSL across all tests and what that DSL should be.

Instead of duplicating code by mixing the same traits together repeatedly, we recommend you create abstract base classes for your project that mixes together the features you use the most. For example, you might create a `UnitSpec` class (not trait, for speedier compiles) for unit tests that look like this:

```
package com.packt
import org.scalatest._
abstract class UnitSpec extends FlatSpec
                        with Matchers
                        with OptionValues
                        with Inside
                        with Inspectors
```

Note that we added a few more traits. We do not have immediate use for these traits, but we will be looking at using them later. We will also need to change all the previously written tests to reuse this base class instead of the original `FlatSpec`, for example:

```
class DecimalBinarySpec extends UnitSpec {...}
class BeanSpec extends UnitSpec (---)
class BinaryToDecimalSpec extends UnitSpec {...}
```

Most projects end up with multiple base classes, each focused on a different kind of test. You might have a base class for integration tests that require a database (perhaps named `DbSpec`), another for integration tests that require an actor system (perhaps named `ActorSysSpec`), and another for integration test that require both a database and an actor system (perhaps named `DbActorSysSpec`), and so on.

Test fixtures

Test fixture is a collection of classes, other libraries, and artifacts. These can be files, sockets, database connections, and so on, that are required for testing. Clean code principles dictate that we reuse these fixtures across tests and make them as abstract as possible. For example, if two tests require speaking to a database, then it would be obvious to reuse the same database connection code for both. It is important to try and avoid duplicating the fixture code across those tests. The more code duplication you have in your tests, the greater drag the tests will have on refactoring the actual.

These are the recommended techniques for reusing the code in ScalaTest:

- Refactor using Scala
- Override `withFixture`
- Mixin a `before-and-after` trait

All of the preceding techniques are geared toward reducing code duplication by reducing dependencies between the tests. Eliminating a shared mutable state across tests will make your test code easier to reason with, and more amenable for parallel test execution.

The following sections describe these techniques, including explaining the recommended usage for each. But first, let's summarize the options:

Refactor using Scala when different tests need different fixtures	
get-fixture methods	The *extract method* refactor helps you create a fresh instance of mutable fixture objects in each test that needs them, but doesn't help you clean them up when you're done.
fixture-content objects	By placing fixture methods and fields into traits, you can easily give each test just the newly created fixtures it needs by mixing together traits. Use this technique when you need *different combinations of mutable fixture objects in different tests*, and don't need to clean up after.
loan-fixture methods	Factor out duplicate code with the *loan pattern* when different tests need different fixtures *that must be cleaned up afterwards*.

Override withFixture when most or all tests need the same fixture	
withFixture(NoArgsTest)	The recommended default approach when most or all tests need the same fixture treatment. This general technique allows you, for example, to perform side effects at the beginning and end of all or most tests, transform the outcome of tests, retry tests, make decisions based on test names, tags, or other test data. Use this technique unless: • Different tests need different fixtures (refactor using Scala instead) • An exception in fixture code should abort the suite, not fail the test (use a *before-and-after* trait instead) • You have objects to pass into tests (override withFixture(*One*ArgTest) instead)
withFixture(OneArgsTest)	Use when you want to pass the same fixture object or objects as a parameter into all or most tests.

Mix in a before-and-after trait when you want an aborted suite, not a failed test, if the fixture code fails.	
BeforeAndAfter	Use this boilerplate buster when you need to perform the same side effects before and/or after tests, rather than at the beginning or end of tests.
BeforeAndAfterEach	Use when you want to *stack traits* that perform the same side effects before and/or after tests, rather than at the beginning or end of tests.

Calling get-fixture methods

The get-fixture methods are used when one or more test requires same mutable fixture objects created and we don't need them cleaned up after using the fixtures. You can call a get-fixture method at the beginning of each test that needs the fixture, storing the returned object or objects in local variables. A get-fixture method returns a new instance of a needed fixture object (or a holder object containing multiple fixture objects), each time it is called. Here's an example:

```
package com.packt.example.getfixture

import org.scalatest.FlatSpec
import collection.mutable.ListBuffer

class ExampleSpec extends FlatSpec {
  def fixture = new {
    val builder = new StringBuilder("ScalaTest is ")
    val buffer = new ListBuffer[String]
  }

  "Testing" should "be easy" in {
    val f = fixture
    f.builder.append("easy!")
    assert(f.builder.toString === "ScalaTest is easy!")
    assert(f.buffer.isEmpty)
    f.buffer += "sweet"
  }
  it should "be fun" in {
    val f = fixture
    f.builder.append("fun!")
    assert (f.builder.toString === "ScalaTest is fun!")
```

```
        assert (f.buffer.isEmpty)
    }
}
```

The `f.` in front of each use of a fixture object provides a visual indication of which objects are part of the fixture, but if you prefer, you can import the members with `import f._` and use the names directly.

If you need to configure fixture objects differently in different tests, you can pass configuration into the get-fixture method, for example, if you could pass in an initial value for a mutable fixture object as a parameter to the get-fixture method.

Instantiating fixture-context objects

An alternate technique that is especially useful when different tests need different combinations of fixture objects is to define the fixture objects as instance variables of fixture-context objects, whose instantiation forms the body of tests. The like get-fixture methods and fixture-context objects are only appropriate if you don't need to clean up the fixtures after using them.

To use this technique, you define instance variables initialized with fixture objects in traits and/or classes; then in each test instantiate an object that contains just the fixture objects needed by the test. Traits allow you to mix together just the fixture objects needed by each test, whereas classes allow you to pass data in via a constructor to configure the fixture objects. Here's an example in which fixture objects are partitioned into two traits, and each test just mixes together the traits it needs:

```
package com.packt.example.fixturecontext

import collection.mutable.ListBuffer
import org.scalatest.FlatSpec

class ExampleSpec extends FlatSpec {

  trait Builder {
    val builder = new StringBuilder("ScalaTest is ")
  }

  trait Buffer {
    val buffer = ListBuffer("ScalaTest", "is")
  }

  // This test needs the StringBuilder fixture
  "Testing" should "be productive" in new Builder {
```

```
    builder.append("productive!")
    assert(builder.toString === "ScalaTest is productive!")
  }
  // This test needs the ListBuffer[String] fixture
  "Test code" should "be readable" in new Buffer {
    buffer += ("readable!")
    assert(buffer === List("ScalaTest", "is", "readable!"))
  }
  // This test needs both the StringBuilder and ListBuffer
  it should "be clear and concise" in new Builder with Buffer {
    builder.append("clear!")
    buffer += ("concise!")
    assert(builder.toString === "ScalaTest is clear!")
    assert(buffer === List("ScalaTest", "is", "concise!"))
  }
}
```

Overriding withFixture(NoArgTest)

Although the get-fixture method and fixture-context object approaches take care of setting up a fixture at the beginning of each test, they don't address the problem of cleaning up a fixture at the end of the test. If you just need to perform a side effect at the beginning or end of a test, and don't need to actually pass any fixture objects into the test, you can override withFixture(NoArgTest), one of ScalaTest's life cycle methods defined in trait Suite.

Trait Suite's implementation of runTest passes a no-arg test function to withFixture(NoArgTest). It is withFixture method's responsibility to invoke that test function. Suite's implementation of withFixture simply invokes the function, as follows:

```
// Default implementation in trait Suite
protected def withFixture(test: NoArgTest) = {
  test()
}
```

You can, therefore, override withFixture to perform a setup before and/or clean up after invoking the test function. If you have cleanup to perform, you should invoke the test function inside a try block and perform the cleanup in a finally clause, in case an exception propagates back through withFixture. (If a test fails because of an exception, the test function invoked by withFixture will result in a failed wrapping the exception. Nevertheless, best practice is to perform clean up in a final clause just in case an exception occurs.)

The `withFixture` method is designed to be stacked; and to enable this, you should always call the super-implementation of `withFixture`, and let it invoke the `test` function rather than invoking the `test` function directly. That is to say, instead of writing `test()`, you should write `super.withFixture(test)`, as follows:

```scala
// Your implementation
override def withFixture(test: NoArgTest) = {
  // Perform setup
  try super.withFixture(test)
  // Invoke the test function
  finally {
    // Perform cleanup
  }
}
```

Here's an example in which `withFixture(NoArgTest)` is used to take a snapshot of the working directory if a test fails, and to send that information to the reporter:

```scala
package com.packt.example.noargtest

import java.io.File
import org.scalatest._

class ExampleSpec extends FlatSpec {
  override def withFixture(test: NoArgTest) = {
    super.withFixture(test) match {
      case failed: Failed =>
        val currDir = new File(".")
        val fileNames = currDir.list()
        info("Dir snapshot: " + fileNames.mkString(", "))
        failed
      case other => other
    }
  }

  "This test" should "succeed" in {
    assert(1 + 1 === 2)
  }

  it should "fail" in {
    assert(1 + 1 === 3)
  }
}
```

Running this version of `ExampleSuite` in the interpreter in a directory with two files, `hello.txt` and `world.txt`, will give the following output:

```
scala> new ExampleSuite execute ExampleSuite:
This test - should succeed - should fail *** FAILED ***
 2 did not equal 3 (<console>:33)
+ Dir snapshot: hello.txt, world.txt
```

Note that the `NoArgTest` passed to `withFixture`, in addition to an `apply` method that executes the test, also includes TestData, such as the test name and the config map passed to runTest. Thus, you can also use the test name and configuration objects in your `withFixture` implementation.

Calling loan-fixture methods

If you need to both pass a fixture object into a test and perform clean up at the end of the test, you'll need to use the *loan pattern*. If different tests need different fixtures that require clean up, you can implement the loan pattern directly by writing **loan-fixture** methods. A loan-fixture method takes a function whose body forms part or all of a test's code. It creates a fixture, passes it to the test code by invoking the function, and then cleans up the fixture after the function returns.

The following example shows three tests that use two fixtures: a database and a file. Both require clean up after, so each is provided via a loan-fixture method. (In this example, the database is simulated with `StringBuffer`):

```scala
package com.packt.examples.loanfixture

import java.util.concurrent.ConcurrentHashMap

object DbServer {
  // Simulating a database server
  type Db = StringBuffer
  private val databases = new ConcurrentHashMap[String, Db]

  def createDb(name: String): Db = {
    val db = new StringBuffer
    databases.put(name, db)
    db
  }

  def removeDb(name: String) {
    databases.remove(name)
  }
```

```scala
}


import org.scalatest.FlatSpec

import DbServer._
import java.util.UUID.randomUUID
import java.io._

class ExampleSpec extends FlatSpec {
  def withDatabase(testCode: Db => Any) {
    val dbName = randomUUID.toString
    val db = createDb(dbName)
    // create the fixture
    try {
      db.append("ScalaTest is ")
      // perform setup
      testCode(db)
      // "loan" the fixture to the test
    }
    finally removeDb(dbName)
    // clean up the fixture
  }

  def withFile(testCode: (File, FileWriter) => Any) {
    val file = File.createTempFile("hello", "world")

    // create the fixture
    val writer = new FileWriter(file)
    try {
      writer.write("ScalaTest is ")
      // set up the fixture
      testCode(file, writer)
      // "loan" the fixture to the test
    }
    finally writer.close()
    // clean up the fixture
  }

  // This test needs the file fixture
  "Testing" should "be productive" in withFile {
    (file, writer) =>
      writer.write("productive!")
      writer.flush()
      assert(file.length === 24)
  }
  // This test needs the database fixture
  "Test code" should "be readable" in withDatabase {
```

```
        db => db.append("readable!")
        assert(db.toString === "ScalaTest is readable!")
    }
    // This test needs both the file and the database
    it should "be clear and concise" in withDatabase {
        db => withFile { (file, writer) =>
            // loan-fixture methods compose
            db.append("clear!")
            writer.write("concise!")
            writer.flush()
            assert(db.toString === "ScalaTest is clear!")
            assert(file.length === 21)
        }
    }
}
```

As demonstrated by the last test, loan-fixture methods compose. Not only do loan-fixture methods allow you to give each test the fixture it needs, they allow you to give a test multiple fixtures and clean everything up afterwards.

Also demonstrated in this example is the technique of giving each test its own "fixture sandbox" to play in. When your fixtures involve external side-effects, such as creating files or databases, it is a good idea to give each file or database a unique name, as is done in this example. This keeps tests completely isolated, allowing you to run them in parallel if desired.

Overriding withFixture(OneArgTest)

If all or most tests need the same fixture, you can avoid some of the boilerplate of the loan-fixture method approach using fixture.FlatSpec and overriding withFixture(OneArgTest). Each test in fixture.FlatSpec takes a fixture as a parameter, allowing you to pass the fixture into the test. You must indicate the type of the fixture parameter by specifying FixtureParam and implement withFixturemethod that takes OneArgTest. This withFixture method is responsible for invoking the one-arg test function, so you can perform any test harness setup before the actual test, or perform any housekeeping or cleanup after the test, invoking and passing the fixture into the test function.

To enable the stacking of traits that define `withFixture(NoArgTest)`; it is a good idea to let `withFixture(NoArgTest)` invoke the `test` function instead of invoking the `test` function directly. To do so, you'll need to convert the `OneArgTest` to a `NoArgTest`. You can do that by passing the fixture object to the the `toNoArgTest` method of `OneArgTest`. In other words, instead of writing `test(theFixture)`, you'd delegate responsibility for invoking the `test` function to the `withFixture(NoArgTest)` method of the same instance by writing:

```
withFixture(test.toNoArgTest(theFixture))
```

Here's a complete example:

```
package com.packt.examples.oneargtest

import org.scalatest.fixture
import java.io._

class ExampleSpec extends fixture.FlatSpec {

  case class FixtureParam(file: File, writer: FileWriter)

  def withFixture(test: OneArgTest) = {
    val file = File.createTempFile("hello", "world") // create the fixture
    val writer = new FileWriter(file)
    val theFixture = FixtureParam(file, writer)

    try {
      writer.write("ScalaTest is ")
      // set up the fixture
      withFixture(test.toNoArgTest(theFixture))
      // "loan" the fixture to the test
    } finally writer.close()
    // clean up the fixture
  }

  "Testing" should "be easy" in {
    f => f.writer.write("easy!")
    f.writer.flush()
    assert(f.file.length === 18)
  }
  it should "be fun" in {
    f => f.writer.write("fun!")
    f.writer.flush()
    assert(f.file.length === 17)
  }
}
```

In this example, the tests actually required two fixture objects, `File` and `FileWriter`. In such situations, you can simply define the `FixtureParam` type to be a tuple containing the objects, or as is done in this example, a case class containing the objects.

Mixing in BeforeAndAfter

In all the shared fixture examples shown so far, the activities of creating, setting up, and cleaning up the fixture objects have been performed *during* the test. This means that if an exception occurs during any of these activities, it will be reported as a test failure. Sometimes, however, you may want setup to happen *before* the test starts, and cleanup *after* the test has completed, so that if an exception occurs during setup or cleanup, the entire suite aborts and no more tests are attempted. The simplest way to accomplish this in ScalaTest is to mixin trait **BeforeAndAfter**. With this trait, you can denote a bit of code to run before each test, using the `before` function and/or after each test using the `after` function, like this:

```
package com.packt.examples.beforeandafter

import org.scalatest._
import collection.mutable.ListBuffer

class ExampleSpec extends FlatSpec with BeforeAndAfter {
  val builder = new StringBuilder
  val buffer = new ListBuffer[String]
  before {
    builder.append("ScalaTest is ")
  }
  after {
    builder.clear()
    buffer.clear()
  }
  "Testing" should "be easy" in {
    builder.append("easy!")
    assert(builder.toString === "ScalaTest is easy!")
    assert(buffer.isEmpty)
    buffer += "sweet"
  }
  it should "be fun" in {
    builder.append("fun!")

    assert(builder.toString === "ScalaTest is fun!")
    assert(buffer.isEmpty)
  }
}
```

Note that the only way before and after code can communicate with test code is via some side-effecting mechanism, commonly by reassigning instance `vars` or by changing the state of mutable objects held from instance `vals` (as in this example). If using instance `vars` or mutable objects held from instance `vals`, you wouldn't be able to run tests in parallel in the same instance of the `test` class unless you synchronized access to the shared, mutable state. This is why ScalaTest's `ParallelTestExecution` trait extends one `InstancePerTest` by running each test in its own instance of the class each test has its own copy of the instance variables so you don't need to synchronize. If you mixed `ParallelTestExecution` into the preceding `ExampleSuite`, the tests would run in parallel just fine without any synchronization needed on the mutable `StringBuilder` and `ListBuffer[String]` objects.

Although `BeforeAndAfter` provides a minimal-boilerplate way to execute code before and after tests, it isn't designed to enable stackable traits, because the order of execution would be non obvious.

Composing fixtures by stacking traits

In larger projects, teams often end up with several different fixtures that `test` classes need in different combinations, and possibly initialized (and cleaned up) in different orders. A good way to accomplish this in ScalaTest is to factor the individual fixtures into traits that can be composed using the *stackable trait* pattern. This can be done, for example, by placing `withFixture` methods in several traits, each of which call `super.withFixture`. Here's an example in which the `StringBuilder` and `ListBuffer[String]` fixtures used in the previous examples have been factored out into two *stackable fixture traits* named `Builder` and `Buffer`:

```
package com.packt.examples.composingwithfixture

import org.scalatest._
import collection.mutable.ListBuffer

trait Builder extends SuiteMixin {
  this: Suite =>
  val builder = new StringBuilder

  abstract override def withFixture(test: NoArgTest) = {
    builder.append("ScalaTest is ")
    try super.withFixture(test)
    // To be stackable, must call super.withFixture
    finally builder.clear()
  }
```

```
  }

trait Buffer extends SuiteMixin {
  this: Suite =>
  val buffer = new ListBuffer[String]

  abstract override def withFixture(test: NoArgTest) = {
    try super.withFixture(test)
    // To be stackable, must call super.withFixture
    finally buffer.clear()
  }
}

class ExampleSpec extends FlatSpec with Builder with Buffer {
  "Testing" should "be easy" in {
    builder.append("easy!")
    assert(builder.toString === "ScalaTest is easy!")
    assert(buffer.isEmpty)
    buffer += "sweet"
  }
  it should "be fun" in {
    builder.append("fun!")
    assert(builder.toString === "ScalaTest is fun!")
    assert(buffer.isEmpty)
    buffer += "clear"
  }
}
```

By mixing in both the `Builder` and `Buffer` traits, `ExampleSuite` gets both fixtures, which will be initialized before each test and cleaned up after. The order the traits are mixed together determines the order of execution. In this case, `Builder` is "super" to `Buffer`. If you wanted `Buffer` to be "super" to `Builder`, you need only switch the order you mix them together, like this:

```
class Example2Suite extends Suite with Buffer with Builder
```

If you only need one fixture, you mixin only that trait:

```
class Example3Suite extends Suite with Builder
```

Another way to create stackable fixture traits is by extending `BeforeAndAfterEach` and/or `BeforeAndAfterAll` traits. `BeforeAndAfterEach` has a `beforeEach` method that will be run before each test (like JUnit's `setUp`), and an `afterEach` method that will be run after (like JUnit's `tearDown`). Similarly, `BeforeAndAfterAll` has a `beforeAll` method that will be run before all tests, and an `afterAll` method that will be run after all tests. Here's what the previously shown example would look like if it were rewritten to use the `BeforeAndAfterEach` methods instead of `withFixture`:

```scala
package com.packt.examples.composingbeforeandaftereach

import org.scalatest._
import collection.mutable.ListBuffer

trait Builder extends BeforeAndAfterEach {
  this: Suite =>
  val builder = new StringBuilder

  override def beforeEach() {
    builder.append("ScalaTest is ")
    super.beforeEach()
    // To be stackable, must call super.beforeEach
  }

  override def afterEach() {
    try super.afterEach()
    // To be stackable, must call super.afterEach
    finally builder.clear()
  }
}

trait Buffer extends BeforeAndAfterEach {
  this: Suite =>
  val buffer = new ListBuffer[String]

  override def afterEach() {
    try super.afterEach()
    // To be stackable, must call super.afterEach
    finally buffer.clear()
  }
}

class ExampleSpec extends FlatSpec with Builder with Buffer {
  "Testing" should "be easy" in {
    builder.append("easy!")
    assert(builder.toString === "ScalaTest is easy!")
    assert(buffer.isEmpty)
    buffer += "sweet"
```

```
    }
    it should "be fun" in {
      builder.append("fun!")
      assert(builder.toString === "ScalaTest is fun!")
      assert(buffer.isEmpty)
      buffer += "clear"
    }
  }
```

To get the same ordering as `withFixture`, place your `super.beforeEach` call at the end of each `beforeEach` method, and the `super.afterEach` call at the beginning of each `afterEach` method, as shown in the previous example. It is a good idea to invoke `super.afterEach` in a `try` block and perform cleanup in a `final` clause, as shown in the previous example, because this ensures the cleanup code is performed even if `super.afterEach` throws an exception.

The difference between stacking traits that extend `BeforeAndAfterEach` versus traits that implement `withFixture` is that setup and cleanup code happens before and after the test in `BeforeAndAfterEach`, but at the beginning and end of the test in `withFixture`. Thus, if a `withFixture` method completes abruptly with an exception, it is considered a failed test. By contrast, if any of the `beforeEach` or `afterEach` methods of `BeforeAndAfterEach` complete abruptly, it is considered an aborted suite, which will result in a `SuiteAborted` event.

Problem statement

We will extend our example from the previous chapter about base conversion so that we can convert from decimal to hexadecimal and vice versa.

Feature – decimal to hexadecimal conversion

As a user, I want to convert a decimal number to a hexadecimal number.

Scenario 1:

- Given a decimal number *A*
- When I convert this number to a hexadecimal number
- Then, I get a hexadecimal equivalent *B* of the original decimal number

Scenario 2:

- Given a hexadecimal number X
- When I convert this number to a decimal number
- Then, I get decimal equivalent Y of the original hexadecimal number

Scenario 3:

- Given a decimal number A
- When I convert A to hexadecimal to get hexadecimal number B
- And I again convert B to decimal number C
- Then, A is equal to C

Let's apply some of the knowledge we gained in this chapter, so we can take another step toward reusable and clean test code for our example application. In TDD, test code is equally if not more important than the application code.

Now that we are looking at reusing some of the test code from our example from previous chapters, we should start by creating a base test class. This has been done in the *Base test class* section of this chapter. We can start writing tests for the new feature and scenarios:

```
package com.packt

class DecimalHexadecimalSpec extends UnitSpec {
  "base conversion utility" should "convert a number 1243
  into a binary number 4DB" in {
    var hex: Hexadecimal =
    BaseConversion.decimalToHexadecimal(Decimal("1243"))
    assert(hex.number == "4DB")
  }
}
```

To get rid of the compilation failures, we can start building the missing classes and methods.

We will add another case class to the `package` object, as shown here:

```
case class Hexadecimal(number:String) extends Number
```

Along with a test for this class in bean spec:

```
"Hexadecimal" should "throw error when
initalised with a non numeric string" in {
  intercept[IllegalArgumentException] {
    Hexadecimal("XYZ")
```

```
    }
  }
```

Similar to the approach taken previously, we will end up with a failing test and an unimplemented method `decimalToHexadecimal` as shown here:

```
def decimalToHexadecimal(decimal: Decimal): Hexadecimal = ???
```

For the sake of being succinct, I will skip some steps in the book and will urge the reader to try them out. We end up with an implementation as follows.

BinaryToDecimalSpec.scala

```scala
package com.packt

class BinaryToDecimalSpec extends UnitSpec {
  "base conversion utility" should "convert binary number
  100100111101 to decimal      equivalent 2365" in {
    var decimal:Decimal =
BaseConversion.binaryToDecimal(Binary("100100111101"))
    decimal.number shouldEqual "2365"
  }

  it should "convert binary number 11110001111110111
  to decimal equivalent 123895" in {
    var decimal:Decimal =
    BaseConversion.bianryToDecimal(Binary("11110001111110111"))
    decimal.number shouldBe "123895"
  }

  it should "convert binary number 100000000000001110000001
  to decimal equivalent 8389505" in {
    var decimal:Decimal =
    BaseConversion.bianryToDecimal(Binary("100000000000001110000001"))
    decimal.number should equal("8389505")
  }
}
```

HexadecimalToDecimalSpec.scala

```scala
package com.packt

class HexadecimalToDecimalSpec extends UnitSpec {
  "base conversion utility" should "convert hexadecimal
  number AB to decimal equivalent 171" in {
    var decimal:Decimal =
```

```
BaseConversion.hexadecimalToBinary(Hexadecimal("AB"))
    decimal.number shouldEqual "171"
  }

  it should "convert hexadecimal number 123AB
  to decimal equivalent 74667" in {
    var decimal:Decimal =
    BaseConversion.hexadecimalToBinary(Hexadecimal("123AB"))
    decimal.number shouldBe "74667"
  }

  it should "convert hexadecimal number ABCDEF
  to decimal equivalent 11259375" in {
    var decimal:Decimal =
    BaseConversion.hexadecimalToBinary(Hexadecimal("ABCDEF"))
    decimal.number should equal("11259375")
  }
}
```

DecimalHexadecimalSpec.scala

```
package com.packt

class DecimalHexadecimalSpec extends UnitSpec {
  "base conversion utility" should "convert a number 1243
  into a hexadecimal number 4DB" in {
    var hex: Hexadecimal =
BaseConversion.decimalToHexadecimal(Decimal("1243"))
    hex.number should be ("4DB")
  }

  it should "convert a number 11111122 into
  a hexadecimal number A98AD2" in {
    var hex: Hexadecimal =
    BaseConversion.decimalToHexadecimal(Decimal("11111122"))
    hex.number should be ("A98AD2")
  }
}
```

BeanSpec.scala

```
package com.packt

class BeanSpec extends UnitSpec {
  "Decimal" should "throw error when initalised
  with a non numeric string" in {
```

```scala
    try {
      Decimal("XYZ")
    }
    catch {
      case e:IllegalArgumentException =>
        assert(e.getMessage == "requirement failed:
        Unable to convert string to number")
      case _ =>fail
    }
  }

  "Binary" should "throw error when initalised
  with a non numeric string" in {
    intercept[IllegalArgumentException] {
      Binary("XYZ")
    }
  }

  "Hexadecimal" should "throw error when initalised
  with a non numeric string" in {
    intercept[IllegalArgumentException] {
      Hexadecimal("XYZ")
    }
  }
}
```

package.scala.packt

```scala
package com

package object packt {

  trait Number {
    def number:String
    require(number forall {c => Character.isDigit(c) ||
    Seq('A', 'B', 'C', 'D', 'E', 'F').contains(c)},
    "Unable to convert string to number")
  }

  case class Decimal(number:String) extends Number

  case class Binary(number:String) extends Number

  case class Hexadecimal(number:String) extends Number

}
```

BaseConversion.scala

```scala
package com.packt

import scala.annotation.tailrec

object BaseConversion {
  val hexTable =
  Array('0','1','2','3','4','5','6','7','8','9','A','B','C','D','E','F')

  def decimalToHexadecimal(decimal: Decimal): Hexadecimal = {
    Hexadecimal(toHexadecimal(BigInt(decimal.number), "").toString)
  }


  def bianryToDecimal(binary: Binary): Decimal = {
    val seq = binary.number.reverse.zipWithIndex.map { case (a, i) =>
      a.toString.toInt * math.pow(2, i) }
    Decimal(seq.sum.toInt.toString)
  }

  def decimalToBinary(decimal: Decimal) = {
    Binary(toBinary(BigInt(decimal.number), "").toString)
  }

  @tailrec
  private def toBinary(num: BigInt, acc: String): String = {
    if (num < 2) (num.toInt + acc)
    else toBinary(num / 2, (num mod 2).toString ++ acc)
  }

  @tailrec
  private def toHexadecimal(num: BigInt, acc: String): String = {
    if (num < 16) (hexTable(num.toInt).toString + acc)
    else toHexadecimal(num / 16, hexTable((num mod 16).toInt).toString ++
acc)
  }
}
```

We used some of the new Matchers we learned in this chapter. We have also replaced the vanilla assertions from the previously written tests with more verbose Matchers.

As an exercise, I would suggest the readers extend the example now to include decimal to octal conversion and vice versa. This implementation will be shown in the next chapter for you to compare your solution.

Summary

There are some obvious issues that we can see in this implementation. Firstly, there is lot of common code that can be reused. Secondly, the require clause in the `Number` trait is not quite fit for purpose now, as effectively we can create `Binary("ABC")` without any exceptions. It would be a good idea to tinker around with the code at this point and try and experiment with the Matchers we have discussed in this chapter.

In the coming chapters, we will look to evolve a fixture. We will also evolve the architecture of our application code gradually with more features being added.

4
Refactor Mercilessly

Refactoring your code is a continuous process. It should not be limited to just the application code. In this chapter we will cover:

- Clean code
- Red-Green-Refactor
- Code smell
- To refactor or not to refactor?
- Refactoring techniques
- Building reusable test code

Clean code

We have been harping on about clean code for a while now. Let's take a moment to define what exactly clean code is.

Very simply put, clean code is simple code: no gimmicks, no short cuts, and easy to understand. It should pass all the tests and should not have any duplication. It contains the minimum number of moving parts.

Red-Green-Refactor

I first heard the term "refactor mercilessly" from the person responsible for hand-holding and inducting me into the Agile process. It was originally coined as part of **eXtreme Programming** (**XP**), which is one of the several popular Agile processes that involve very short iterations, continuous releases, and paired-programming. After spending more than a decade with these processes, I can undoubtedly say that there is no way to refactor other than mercilessly. You can't do it half-heartedly or incompletely, as it accumulates as tech debt, but at some stage there is no other way but to do a big bang refactoring exercise. If you have been using Agile previously then you would know how easy it is to ignore refactoring and then end up going through a massive refactoring story to clear up the technical debt.

It is always recommended that you take into account the refactoring effort as part of the story estimation process.

Refactoring is the last straw in our test-driven cycle (Red-Green-Refactor), just before we go back to writing another failing test. The fact that refactoring comes in after the Green, that is, a passing test, is important. At the point we refactor, we are sure that the code we have written is sufficient to fulfill the assumption in our test and is transitively fulfilling the acceptance criteria of the story. Keeping this in mind, when we refactor our code, our end goal after refactoring is to keep the tests Green so that the functionality is still working. This gives us a boundary to play within. We can refactor mercilessly within the bounds that the tests should still pass.

The refactoring, though, is not limited to application code alone. Test code needs to be refactored as well. Reusability and clean code form the cornerstones of any refactoring effort. Most refactoring is just common sense, but there are some refactoring techniques that we can discuss here, and they can act as a trigger for you to know what can be refactored. Before we get onto the refactoring techniques, let us discuss code smells.

Code smell

Code smell in the source code is any indication on the surface of the programming code that hints at a deeper problem. This can be as trivial as an oversized method. The most accurate indication of a code smell is the testability of the code. If the code can be tested in a very simple and straightforward test then that means the code is not tightly coupled. This also means that the code is doing only one task, which can be tested end to end.

"a code smell is a surface indication that usually corresponds to a deeper problem in the system"

– Martin Fowler

There are a few types of code smell that can be identified by looking at the code.

Expendable

An **expendable** is something gratuitous and futile. Removal of such code will make the code cleaner, efficient, and comprehensible. It can be one of the following:

- **Comments**: As programmers, we sometimes tend to do things in the most cryptic way possible and then write lines of comments around the code to explain what ingenious solution we have come up with. This leads to code that is weaved around comments. My personal belief is that code should be self-documented and that the tests should act as the documentation of the code. For this to happen, the code needs to be very simple to understand.

- **Code duplication**: Code duplication is the most obvious of the code smells and the source of all evil. Any time you see the same code being written multiple times in your application code base, it reeks. The duplicate code does not mean it is the same code in the syntax; it can be a duplication of functionality as well. For example, two classes may be creating a connection to the same database in two different ways.

- **Insignificant classes**: This is a little hard to detect, but any class that is doing little or has a very insignificant task is a code smell. In most cases, this can just be given an inline class treatment, which we will discuss later.

- **Unreachable and dead code**: This can be the residue of refactoring or just bad programming. Most of the new IDEs are quite good at identifying unreachable code. Dead code can be a variable, field, method, or class that is no longer required.

- **Hypothetical platitude**: Sometimes we get so involved with the functionality in our implementation that we end up writing code to futureproof our implementation. This means that we write code to support anticipated future changes that may never happen. There is an acronym for it: **YAGNI (You Ain't Gonna Need It)**.

Couplers

These code smells contribute towards excessive coupling between classes. This makes the classes untestable in isolation. These smells are:

- **Feature envy**: If your method is making extensive use of another class then it would mean that this method should belong in the other class it is envious of.
- **Inappropriate intimacy**: When your class is using internal fields and methods of another class. This violates the rule of encapsulation.
- **Function chaining**: When you see multiple functions chained together like `a.b().c().d()`, then it means that the client is responsible for navigation along the class structure, resulting in smell.
- **Broker class**: If the class is designed to delegate functionality to another class then maybe this class is not required at all.

Modification thwarters

- **Deviating modification**: When you find yourself changing many unrelated methods when changing a class. This is mostly a result of "copy-paste programming".
- **Shotgun surgery**: If to make one small change you have to make changes to many different classes, this means that the responsibility has been split up among a number of classes.
- **Parallel inheritance hierarchies**: Whenever you create a subclass for a class, and you end up having to create a subclass of one or more other classes too.

Bloaters

Bloaters are methods or classes that have increased to such monstrous proportions that they are very hard to work with:

- **Long method**: The general rule of thumb is that any method longer than 10 lines of code is a code smell.
- **Large class**: This is a class containing many fields and methods. Ideally a class should be around 200 at the most.

- **Primitive obsession**: When your code uses primitive types rather than small objects, or constants, for information or as field names. Just as with many other smells, this arises because of moments of weakness, when you just need a field to store some data.
- **Long parameter list**: When your method requires more than three or four parameters. This may mean several algorithms are merged in a single method.
- **Data clumps**: Sometimes different parts of code contain identical groups of variables, for example, when connecting to a database. These are candidates for moving into their own classes.

Object-oriented abusers

All these smells arise from inappropriate or incomplete use of object-oriented principles:

- **Switch statement**: When you have a complex `switch` statement or a very long nested `if` statement, you need to revisit your code with a polymorphic solution.
- **Temporary fields**: Temporary fields get their value only under certain circumstances. If these circumstances don't occur, then these fields are empty. Use of these fields makes your code very hard to understand.
- **Refused bequest**: When some or most of the functionality inherited by the subclass is not used, it means the classes (parent and child) are unrelated. In such cases, inheritance should be eliminated for some other approach, such as composition or delegation.
- **Alternative classes with different interfaces**: This occurs more often than you would think—when two of the classes perform the same functionality but their method names are different. This is mostly a result of poor communication between the team where some developers do not know if a class already exists to provide this functionality and end up creating a new one.

Obsolete libraries

Sometimes the third-party libraries you are using are not updated so often and become obsolete in some respects. You may be tempted to write your own libraries, and that would be a code smell as you are reinventing the wheel. In such cases, though the library code is read only, there are techniques that we can use to extend functionality to fulfill our needs.

To refactor or not to refactor

There is no such thing as too much refactoring, but there are stages in the development process that act as an impetus for refactoring. Here are a few of them.

Doing it thrice (rule of three)

When you do something the first time, you just do it to get it done. When doing the same thing a second time, you do the same thing again, though you squirm at having to repeat it. When you do it a third time, you start refactoring.

Adding new feature

When you are adding a new feature to someone else's unclear code, it is better to start refactoring it before adding the feature. Refactoring helps you understand the unclear code. Refactored code facilitates the smooth addition of new features.

Bug fixing

Bugs normally live in smelly code. They both go hand in hand. Once you start refactoring your code, most of the bugs just jump out into the open.

Code reviews

Many organizations now use a tier of code review exercise which can be done by peers. If any code smells become apparent during the code review exercises, it should be taken up for refactoring proactively.

Refactoring techniques

Though it's fair to say refactoring is more about common sense than a technique, there are still some very obvious refactoring techniques. The first step is to identify the code smell, which we covered in the previous section. The list is not exhaustive but just covers some frequently occurring pitfalls. Let's discuss the refactoring techniques that we can use to eliminate these code smells.

Composing methods

The majority of the code smells discussed earlier arise from within the method. The following refactoring techniques help to streamline the code and remove duplication:

- **Extract method**: Whenever you see a code fragment that can be grouped together and/or does not belong in its current place, this code can be extracted into its own method.

  Before refactoring:

  ```
  def printReport() {
     printBanner()
     println("Next line of report")
     println("Another line of report")
  }
  ```

  After refactoring:

  ```
  def printReport() {
     printBanner()
     printRestOfIt()
  }

  def printRestOfIt() {
     println("Next line of report")
     println("Another line of report")
  }
  ```

- **Inline method**: When a method delegates a very trivial job to another method, this results in a tangle of methods. This can be resolved by inlining the code of the called method into the calling method.

  Before refactoring:

  ```
  def getPrice() = buyingMoreThan5() ? 100:150

  def buyingMoreThan5() = quantity > 5
  ```

  After refactoring:

  ```
  def getPrice() = quantity > 5 ? 100:150
  ```

- **Extract variable**: When you have an expression that is hard to understand, extract it into a variable with a name that defines the expression.

  Before refactoring:

  ```
  def calculateGrade(person:Person)  =
     if(person.profile.gender == "Male"
       && person.report.sumOfScore > 80)
         "A"
     else
         "B"
  ```

  After refactoring:

  ```
  def calculateGrade(person:Person)  {
     val isMale = person.profile.gender == "Male"
     val scoreMoreThan80 = person.report.sumOfScore > 80
     if(isMale && scoreMoreThan80)
         "A"
     else
         "B"
  }
  ```

- **Inline temp**: This is the opposite of the `extract` variable, in that if the expression in the `temp` variable is too trivial and readable it will make sense to get rid of it.

  Before refactoring:

  ```
  def giveFree(person:Person) {
     val isMinor = person.isMinor
     isMinor
  }
  ```

  After refactoring:

  ```
  def giveFree(person:Person)  =  person.isMinor
  ```

- **Replace temp with query**: Sometimes we have temporary variables holding the results of an expression. These expressions can be extracted into a method, thus making it reusable and reducing the size of the original method.

  Before refactoring:

  ```
  def discountedAmount() {
     val total = quantity * price
     if(total > 100)
         total * 0.95
  ```

```
        else
            total * 0.98
    }
```

After refactoring:

```
def discountedAmount() {
    if(getTotal > 100)
        getTotal * 0.95
    else
        getTotal * 0.98
}

def getTotal = quantity * price
```

- **Replace method with method object**: When you have a long method with intertwined calculations that are not easy to extract to a method, then you can extract the method into its own object, where the local variables will become fields and the method can be split into multiple methods.

Before refactoring:

```
def price() {
    val primaryBasePrice;
    val secondaryBasePrice;
    val tertiaryBasePrice;
    // long computation.
    //...
}
```

After refactoring:

```
object Order {
    val primaryBasePrice;
    val secondaryBasePrice;
    val tertiaryBasePrice;

    def priceCalculator() {
        ....
    }

    def compute() {
        ....
    }
}
```

- **Substitute algorithm**: When you want to replace an existing algorithm with a new one, you can just replace the body of the method that implements the algorithm.

  Before refactoring:

  ```
  def someMethod(){
      // ....
          .... old algorithm
      ...
      //
      doSomething()
  }
  ```

After refactoring:

```
def someMethod(){
    // ....
        .... new improved algorithm
    ...
    //
    doSomething()
}
```

Moving features between objects

These refactoring techniques are used when you have distributed functionality between different classes. Some of these techniques are:

- **Move method**: When a method is used more in another class than the class it is in, it would make perfect sense to move this method to this second class where it is used the most. You can delete the original method altogether or keep a reference to this newly moved method in the original method:

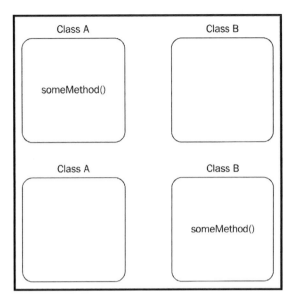

- **Move field**: If a field is used more in another class than the class it is created in, we can move the field in the class that uses it most and redirect all references from the old field to the new one:

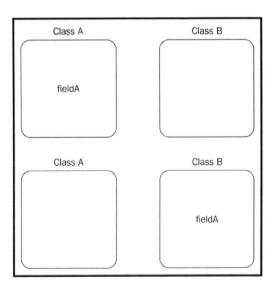

- **Extract class**: If a class is containing the functionality of two classes, we can create a new class that can contain this additional functionality from the first class.

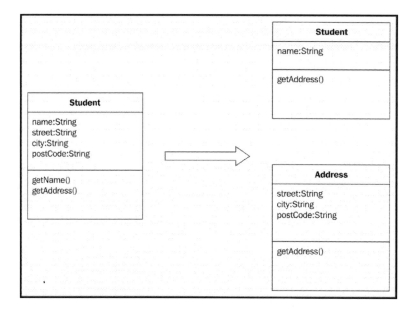

- **Inline class**: When one class does little or nothing such that it can be absorbed into another class:

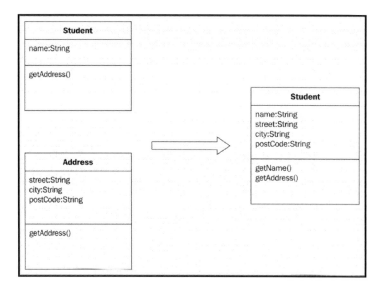

- **Hide delegate**: When a client class makes a call to a method in class *A* and then uses the value returned to call a method in class *B*, we can simplify this by making class *A* call class *B* and return the final value to the client class:

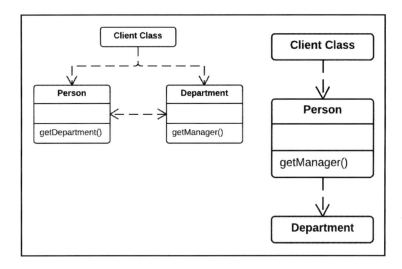

- **Remove middle man**: This is almost the opposite of hiding the delegate, where if you have too many methods that delegate to other objects, you can delete these methods and force the client to call the end point directly:

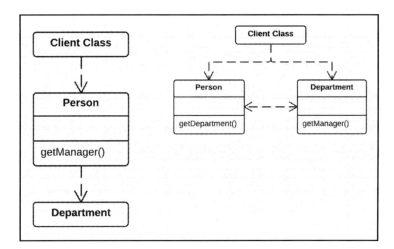

- **Introduce foreign method**: When a utility class you are using does not contain the method you need, you can introduce a method in your class that does the job and also takes the utility class as a parameter.

Before refactoring:

```
object Report {
   //...
   def getReport() {
      //...
      var nextDay = Date(previousDay.getYear, previousDay.getMonth,
        previousDay.getDay + 1)
      // ...
   }
}
```

After refactoring:

```
object Report {
   //...
   def getReport() {
      //...
      var startDate = nextDay(previousDay)
      // ...
   }

   def nextDay(date:Date) {
     Date(previousDay.getYear, previousDay.getMonth,
       previousDay.getDay + 1)
   }
}
```

- **Introduce local extensions**: This technique resolves similar problem to the one solved by introducing a foreign method. If a utility class does not have a few methods that we need, then we can add all these methods to a new class that can either extend the original utility class or acts as wrapper on it:

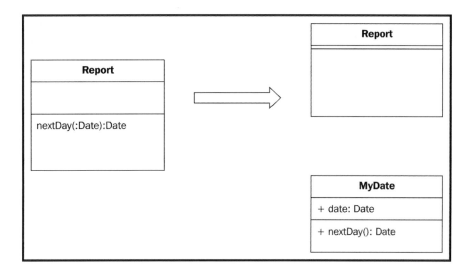

Organizing data

These refactoring techniques help in streamlining data handling. We will only skim over the techniques that are not relevant to Scala. These techniques are:

- **Self-encapsulate field**: If direct access is required to a private field of a class then we can introduce getters and setters for the private field.

Before refactoring:

```scala
class Foo(private val _title: String) {
    def printTitle(b: Book) {
        println(b._title)
    }
}
```

After refactoring:

```scala
class Book(private val _title: String) {
    def title = _title
    def printTitle(b: Book) {
        println(b.title)
    }
}
```

- **Replace data value with object**: If a class contains a data field that has its own behavior and data, we can create a new class and move the field and its behaviors into the new class:

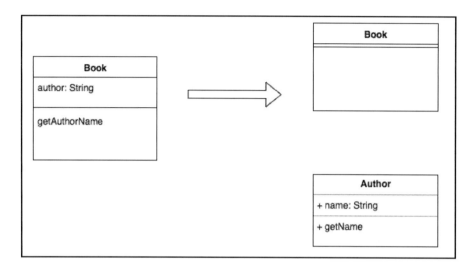

- **Change value to reference**: When there are many identical instances of the same class, they can all be replaced with a single reference object:

- **Change reference to value**: If the reference object is too insignificant to have a life cycle of its own, then it is better to turn it into a value object:

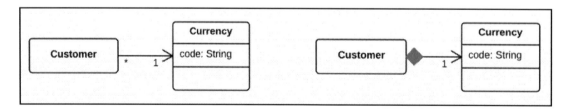

- **Replace array with object**: If you have an array with various types of data, you can replace it with a more meaningful object:

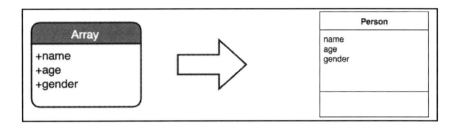

- **Duplicate observed data**: If domain data is used to render the GUI, then it is a good idea to separate this data into a separate class:

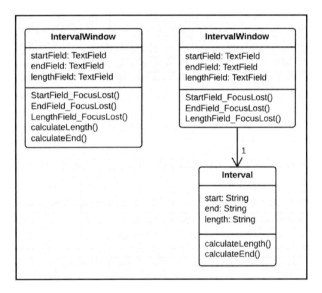

- **Change unidirectional association to bidirectional**: When two classes use features of each other, but there is only a unidirectional relationship between them, then it would be better to turn the relationship into bidirectional:

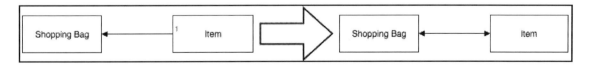

- **Change bidirectional relationship to unidirectional**: If you have a bidirectional relationship between two classes, but only one of the class is using the features of the other class, then it would be better to make the relationship unidirectional:

- **Replace magic number with symbolic constant**: If there is a number that is used within the code and has some meaning to the code, then it is better to give a symbolic name to the number.

Before refactoring:

```
def area(radius:Double) = 2 * 3.14159 * radius
```

After refactoring:

```
val PI = 3.14159
def area(radius:Double) = 2 * PI * radius
```

- **Replace type code with a class**: When you have a set of numbers or strings that forms a list of values which should be allowed as part of the entity:

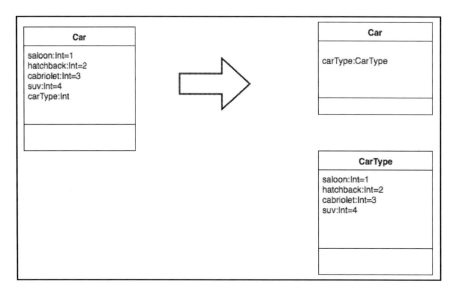

Summary

This chapter has focused entirely on refactoring. We have touched on the importance of refactoring. We have also discussed the various code smells that can be cleared up with refactoring. We have also discussed the stages in the life cycle when refactoring can be undertaken. It is something that should be done at the earliest possible time. Refactoring also completes the test-driven life cycle of Red-Green-Refactor, just before it starts again.

We touched upon various refactoring techniques, focusing in particular on the ones that are relevant to programming in Scala. It would be a good idea to go through the example application code and compare our code to see what can be refactored.

5
Another Level of Testing

 Unit testing is just one aspect of Test-Driven Development. At one point or another, your class will need to interact with other classes inside the application or with other systems outside the ecosystem of your application. In this chapter, we will look at other testing processes that help test the integration and functional aspects of the application. We will be covering the following topics:

- Integration testing
- Behavior-driven development

Integration testing

Individual components of the software module are tested together during integration testing. This phase sits in between unit testing and acceptance testing. In unit testing, we are testing a single unit of the code, whether it be a class or a method. Once we are sure that the individual bits are working according to the specification, we can start with integration testing to check if the modules/components behave as expected with other components, both internal and external.

The process of integration testing can be broken down into these steps:

1. Identify the interfaces between the units that are used for interaction.
2. Specify a collection of units with interfaces that form a complete end-to-end integration.
3. Create integration test cases along with the inputs and expected outputs.
4. Evaluate the test to determine if the results are matched and record the results.

Functional testing

We can think of functional testing as a verification activity. It is a type of black-box testing. The test cases for functional testing are based on the functional requirements of the software system being tested. Functional testing has the end goal of verifying that the software system is functioning according to the design specifications.

When we say that functional testing is black-box testing, it means that the software is tested functionally by providing inputs and comparing the output with the expected output. This does not imply that we are testing a function (method) of the application; it means we are testing a portion of the functionality.

Steps involved in functional testing:

1. Identify the functionality to be tested.
2. Create test data.
3. Ascertain the expected output.
4. Execute the test case.
5. Compare output with the expected outcome.
6. Collate results.

Acceptance testing

Acceptance testing is more focused on the end customer. It means that the application is tested from the point of view of the customer. In some cases, the customer is involved in this testing and the testing is done in a live-like environment that is as close as possible to the actual production system.

During acceptance testing, each user requirement is tested using a test case that focuses on the objectiveness, implementation, error handling, and other details specific to user needs.

Need for user acceptance testing

Even though the application has undergone unit, integration, and functional testing, there can always be a disparity between the customer's view of the application and the developer's or QA's view of the same application.

When developers write their tests they take their own understanding of the requirement into consideration. They may or may not be same as what the customer had asked for. This may as well be a result of miscommunication or lack of a common language between customer and developer.

More often than not, it is the requirements that have evolved, and this change may not have been effectively communicated. It is always nicer to find out these discrepancies well before the application goes into a production environment.

The following are the steps in user acceptance testing:

1. Analyze business requirements.
2. Create a UAT test plan.
3. Identify test scenarios.
4. Create UAT test cases.
5. Prepare test data (production-like data).
6. Run the test cases.
7. Record the results.

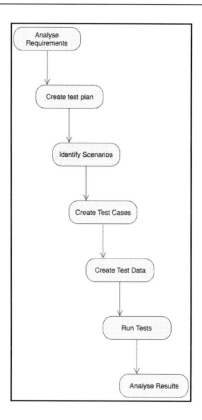

Behavior-driven development

Behavior-driven development (BDD) is the new buzzword in the modern software industry dictionary. It is supposed to be the king of testing techniques. Whether or not this stands up to the hype is yet to be seen, but we have seen some significant improvements in the development process, overall success of the product.

Introduction

In 2007, Sweden commissioned a budget around 10 billion SEK for the development of a dental health service system that was given the name FÃ¶rsÃ¤kringskassan SAP. In 2010, it was realized that the product was not fit for purpose, not on time, and running majorly over budget. Therefore, this project was scrapped. Both outsourced and insourced partners both ended up suing each other.

This is just one instance of the millions of projects costing trillions of dollars that have ended up in a disaster. This happens a lot in the software industry. It has been estimated that nearly half of software projects fail to deliver in one way or another.

The need for BDD stem from these issues. BDD endeavors to focus the major chunk of effort into things that matter the most. It aims at looking objectively at the features that hold the maximum business value and delivering them in the most cost-effective way.

BDD is not an alternative for any of the development processes, but as you will notice in this chapter, it builds on top of these processes to make them better.

Three amigos

The key to BDD is having the customer, developer, and tester involved from the start till the end. So involved, in fact that the three of them sit together and define a common language (ubiquitous language) that is understandable to all three sides. From there onwards, every requirement is translated into this language and the development starts from the premise set by this translated feature.

This model is often referred to as the "three amigos" or the "power of three". Three in this context refer to the customer (or the business analyst sitting in as a proxy for the customer), the developer, and QA. All three bring different kinds of expertise and points of view to the table. The customer brings in their business knowledge and a clear idea of what they want the feature to do. The developer brings in the technical expertise to steer the customer's expectations and the overall application design so that neither the customer is led to believe in the "Promised Land" nor is the developer asked to develop an improbable solution. QA helps put both the customer's requirements and the developer's technical specifications into a format that can be easily tested and verified.

Bird's-eye view of BDD

Let us look at an example of a typical development process, to see where BDD fits in. Let's say Phil's company wants a new feature added to their current payroll system because of some changes in the legislation. The process will go something like this:

1. Phil tells the business analyst how he would like the feature to work.
2. The business analyst will translate Phil's requirements into technical stories or specifications for the developer.

3. The developer will translate these technical requirements into Scala (for the purpose of this book) code and makes sure that his code is bullet proof by writing unit tests.

4. QA will translate the requirements into test cases and will make sure that the code written by the developer satisfies these test cases.

5. The technical writer will translate the application code into documentation.

There are many points in this process where information can get lost.

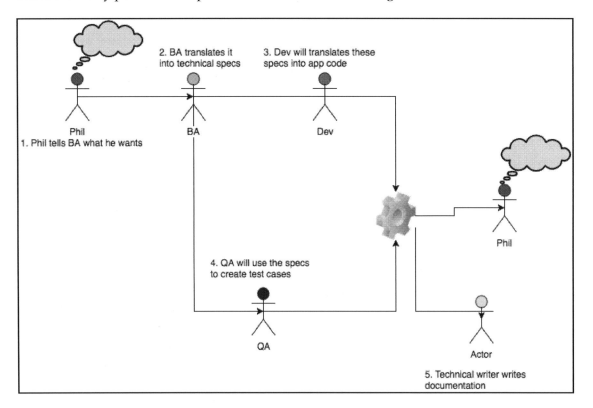

You can see that since everyone works on their own and more or less does their own translation, there are chances of misinterpretation or over-engineering at every point. Now let's suppose that Phil's company is using BDD. Let us see what this process will look like:

1. Phil talks to the BA, telling him what he needs to be built. To remove any misunderstanding, specific examples of the feature are given.

2. Before any development takes place, the three amigos (Dev, QA, and BA) will get together to translate these requirements into scenarios. Scenarios are written in a language which has been agreed upon by Phil, BA, Dev, and QA as being

understandable to all. There is a constant back and forth communication with Phil at this point to iron out any kinks in the understanding of the feature. The ubiquitous language is also referred to as "Gherkin".

3. The developer will turn these scenarios into a set of automation tests. These tests mark the boundaries and requirements of the feature and can be used to determine if the feature is finished.

4. QA uses the scenarios and automation tests as a starting point for writing test cases.

5. The developer will write the application code so that all the automation tests are being passed.

6. The automation tests and scenarios also act as low-level documentation of the system. They can give good examples of how the system should work.

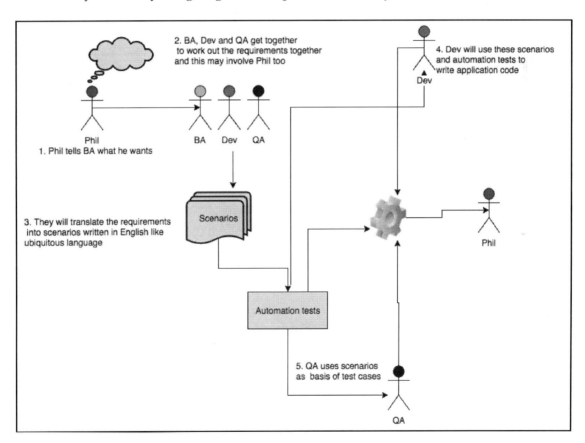

It can be seen that the BDD process is more collaborative. Everyone works together to translate the requirements into a more English-like language that can be understood at all levels. Everyone is on the same page for all the requirements. These requirements also minimize the risk of over-engineering the product, and development effort is limited by the boundaries set by the scenario-driven automation tests. These scenarios, written in the ubiquitous language, will also act as documentation and removes the need for copious documentation accompanying the product. Phil is also involved in the process, and at any point he can check on what is being built for him by reading the scenarios. If at any point he disagrees with it, he can ask for immediate changes rather than waiting for a non-performing and unusable system to be built, with money wasted.

Gherkin

Nearly all of the BDD tools in the market use an English-like format to define the requirements and drive the automated acceptance tests. This format is designed so that all the stakeholders, such as businesses, developers, business analysts, and QAs can easily understand it. This format is called "Gherkin". Strictly speaking, Gherkin refers to the format used by the Cucumber family of BDD tools, but it has become so common that it is even possible to write JBehave acceptance tests that are driven by Gherkin.

Cucumber is a BDD framework that supports many different platforms. In Cucumber you can write integration tests by writing very high-level specifications that describe the application code. These high-level specifications are in plain text. More details about Cucumber can be found at https://cucumber.io/.

JBehave is another very popular framework for BDD. It is, however (as the name suggests), more closely interwoven with Java and related languages (such as Scala). More in-depth information about JBEhave is available at http://jbehave.org/.

In Gherkin, the fundamental requirement is that the same features stay together in the same file called a **feature** file. This feature file contains a brief description of the feature followed by a list of all the scenarios. These scenarios are also the documentation of how the feature works and what the intended behavior should be for each of the features.

We have used Gherkin to write scenarios for our example application built in Chapter 2, *First Test-Driven Application* and Chapter 3, *Clean Code Using ScalaTest*. Here is a very generic format that can be used as a template for writing features in Gherkin:

```
Feature: Some terse yet descriptive text of what is desired
    In order to realize a named business value
    As an explicit system actor
    I want to gain some beneficial outcome that furthers the goal

    Scenario: Some determinable business situation
        Given some precondition
          And some other precondition
        When some action by the actor
          And some other action
          And yet another action
        Then some testable outcome is achieved
          And something else we can check happens too

    Scenario: A different situation
        ...
```

For example:

```
Feature: Payroll generation
    In order to determine the correct remuneration for an employee
    As an explicit system HR manager
    I want to generate correct payroll for the employee

    Scenario: When employee has some unpaid holidays
        Given an employee Jairus
          And Jairus has taken 10 days unpaid leaves
        When HR manager generates his payroll
          And payroll is generated for the month of February 2016
        Then a correct payroll is generated
          And the salary has deductions for the unpaid holidays

    Scenario: When employee has no holidays
        ...
```

Feature files are normally saved with the .feature extension. It can be seen in the last example that although Gherkin requirements are given in plain English, there is a certain structure. Every scenario is made up of a number of steps. Each step starts with one of the keywords (**Given, When, Then, And,** and **But**):

- **Given** defines the precondition for the scenario. This is used to prepare the test environment or prime the data.
- **When** describes the action taken by the actor.

- **Then** describes the expected results or behavior.

Gherkin also allows several correlated scenarios to be congregated into a single scenario that is driven by a table of inputs. This is called a scenario outline. For example:

```
Scenario Outline: Calculate sum
  Given I have two numbers <number-one> and <number-two>
  When these numbers are added
  Then I should have the correct total <sum>
  Examples:
  | number-one | number-two | sum
  | 10000 | 20000 | 30000
  | 10000 | 40000 | 50000
```

Executable specification

These features written in Gherkin form the executable specification that is driven through step definition. **Step definition** is the code that runs behind the steps. In a more mature test harness there is little or no need to write the step definition, as there is enough of it already. Therefore, as long as the same or similar language is used, most of the steps in the feature specification will be covered.

This executable specification is closer to the natural language than the test cases written during acceptance testing, integration testing, or unit testing, for that matter. This makes it a candidate to act as an example of how the application code should be used. This is also a documentation of the collective understanding of the requirements.

Don't repeat yourself

When using BDD, there can be instances where you end up repeating the same test in both the specification level and the unit level. There are different schools of thought regarding how much should be tested at the unit level and how much should be tested at the specification level.

One school of thought believes that you should document as much as possible in specifications while having the minimum possible unit tests. This group of developers believes that all or most of the tests should be documented in a way that can be communicable to the business. This can be visualized as an inverted trapezoid:

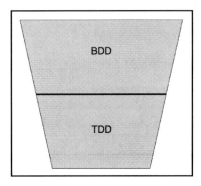

Another school of thought believes in having only the acceptance criteria in the BDD specification and having extensive unit test coverage. This group of developers believes that the tests should be targeted as close to the actual code as possible. This can be imagined as a trapezoid:

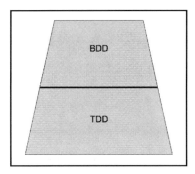

Both these approaches have their merits and demerits and neither is wrong. It is up to the reader to find a middle ground. I am an advocate of having more unit tests and having an adequate number of specifications so that all the functionality of the application code is documented. My reason being is that there is less infrastructure code required for running the unit tests, whereas, in order to run the scenarios, there is a small number (if not a lot) of fixtures that need to be initialized.

A Scala test allows the unit tests to be written in a way that forms an interleaved step definition. Ardent BDD crusaders who write their unit tests in BDD style can use this.

There are, again, two different schools of thought regarding how BDD should be used. One school (the BDD crusaders) believes that the application code should be written inside out to fulfill the BDD scenarios, and, in the end, this should reach unit tests. This means that we write BDD scenarios and then write minimal application code to fulfill the scenarios. Then we add more scenarios and write more application code to satisfy these scenarios. Unit tests are filled in wherever necessary, but BDD is followed in the same manner as TDD, that is, Red-Green-Refactor. With this approach, at any time when we have Green tests, both the unit tests and BDD scenarios are passing. Refactoring is done at all levels and as mercilessly as possible.

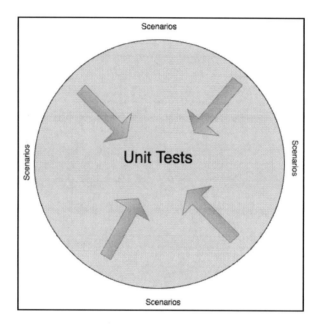

The other school of thought (the TDD worshipers), believe that after writing the BDD scenarios, the application should be built inside outâ◉◉that is, we should write the application code using TDD and then build up the application so that the end goal is that the BDD scenarios are fulfilled. In this approach, we can have unit tests that are passing, but the BDD scenarios will still not be passing as the TDD is still underway.

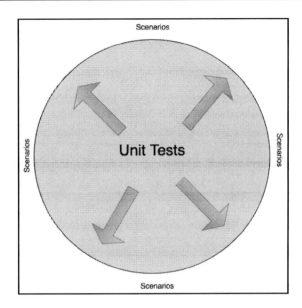

I am a traditionalist and like the second approach, though it can be easily argued that the first approach is comparable (if not better). Therefore, it is left to the reader to determine which approach suits their development style. It may be a matter of trying out both and determining which one is more suitable, or in some cases which approach would work out better than the other.

Talk is cheap

We have talked enough about BDD. There is no alternative to getting our hands on the steering wheel. Let us look at setting up BDD scenarios in our example application using Cucumber.

We will need to introduce the Cucumber library dependencies that we will need to include in our SBT-build descriptor. Along with Cucumber, we will also need dependencies for JUnit. This is because I have always found it easier to integrate Cucumber with SBT using JUnit. There are some third-party SBT plugins that also allow for Cucumber and SBT integration, but since they are not maintained by LightBend (previously known as TypeSafe), they are not up-to-date with the latest Scala and SBT versions.

Adding Cucumber dependency

With the new library dependencies added, our `build.scala` file should look like this:

```
name := "BaseConversionAPI" version := "1.0" scalaVersion := "2.11.8"
libraryDependencies += "org.scalatest" %% "scalatest" % "2.2.6" % "test"
libraryDependencies +="info.cukes" %% "cucumber-scala" % "1.2.4" % "test"
libraryDependencies +="info.cukes" % "cucumber-junit" % "1.2.4" % "test"
libraryDependencies +="junit" % "junit" % "4.11" % "test"
```

For more information about Cucumber, please visit `https://cucumber.io/`.

At the time of writing this book, the latest version of Cucumber dependencies is 1.2.4.

Please refer to `https://cucumber.io/docs/reference/jvm#scala` to find out the latest version to use.

Once these changes have been saved to the `build.sbt` descriptor, the dependencies should be automatically pulled in if you are using an IDE, such as IntelliJ or Eclipse. If you are using a command line, then you may have to run `sbt compile` for SBT to fetch these dependencies.

In IntelliJ, all the external dependencies that have been introduced through the `build` descriptor can be seen inside the **External Libraries** drop-down under the project explorer:

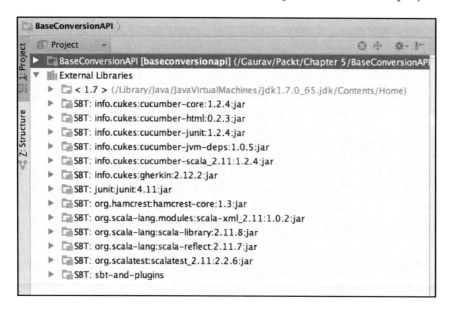

Directory structure

Next, we create the directory where we will keep all our feature files. I suggest creating a folder, named `features`, under `src/main/test`:

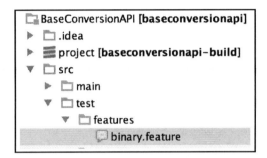

The feature file

As can be seen in the previous figure, we have created a file called `binary.feature` under this directory. This is our first BDD feature file. If this were a strict BDD project this would have been the starting point of our project. At this point, we would have had *three amigos* huddle and come up with the detailed feature that would document the business needs.

As a starting point, we have added this scenario to our `binary.feature` file:

```
Feature: Binary conversions

    Scenario Outline: Binary to decimal conversion
        Given I have a binary number <bin>
        When I convert it to decimal using the BaseConversion utility
        Then I get back a decimal number <dec>
    Examples:
        | bin                          | dec      |
        | 100100111101                 | 2365     |
        | 11110001111110111            | 123895   |
        | 100000000000001110000001     | 8389505  |

    Scenario Outline: Decimal to binary conversion
        Given I have a decimal number <dec>
        When I convert it to binary using the BaseConversion utility
        Then I get back a binary number <bin>
    Examples:
        | dec      | bin                      |
        | 2365     | 100100111101             |
        | 123895   | 11110001111110111        |
```

```
| 8389505 | 100000000000001110000001 |
```

This feature quite precisely and succinctly captures our requirements in a format that can be both understood by the customer and allows it to be parsed by step definitions. We have made use of the scenario outline that allows the introduction of a table of examples. The outline of the scenario is run for each row of the `Examples` table.

Running the feature

To run the feature, just right click anywhere inside the feature file and select `Run: 'Feature: binary'`.

This will result in failed features tests, and show something like this:

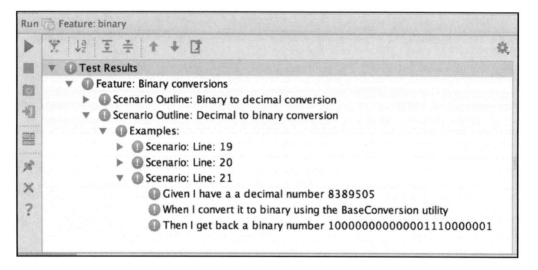

These failures are there because we do not have a step definition file. If you look at the detailed failure messages, you will see something along these lines:

Undefined step: Given I have a binary number 100100111101

Undefined step: When I convert it to decimal using the BaseConversion utility

Undefined step: Then I get back a decimal number 2365

...

Step definition

To create a step definition file, start by creating a directory structure under `src/test/scala` where we can create the step definitions. To do this, create directory (package structure) `support/steps` under `src/test/scala`.

A step definition is the *glue* that binds Gherkin scenarios to the main application code. We have discussed base classes in earlier chapter, as the means of organizing our code. Let us start with a base class for our step definition:

```
package support.steps
import cucumber.api.scala.{EN, ScalaDsl}
import org.scalatest.Matchers
trait BaseSteps extends ScalaDsl with EN with Matchers  {
}
```

We are extending ScalaDsl and EN traits from the Cucumber API and generic Matchers from ScalaTest.

We have tried to make the step definition as generic as possible. It looks something like this:

```
package support.steps

import com.packt.{BaseConversion, Binary, Decimal, Number}

class BaseConversionSteps extends BaseSteps {
  var baseFrom:Number = null
  var baseTo:Number = null

  Given("""^I have a (binary|decimal) number (\d+)$"""){
    (x:String, baseFromNumber:String) =>
      baseFrom = if (x=="binary") Binary(baseFromNumber) else
    Decimal(baseFromNumber)
  }

  When("""^I convert it to (binary|decimal) using
    the BaseConversion utility$"""){ (x:String) =>
      baseTo = if(x=="binary") BaseConversion.decimalToBinary(baseFrom)
else
        BaseConversion.binaryToDecimal(baseFrom)
  }

  Then("""^I get back a (binary|decimal) number
    (\d+)$"""){ (x:String, expected: String) =>
      baseTo.number shouldBe expected
  }
}
```

You can see from this implementation that to make it work, we will have to make changes to the `BaseConversion` API so that all the conversion methods will take a generic `Number` type as a parameter. This is a refactoring that has been driven by our tests. In future examples, we will in future examples refactor more in these lines so that we have a very generic conversion class that is able to convert between different bases. This will be done when we have enough tests (behavioral and unit) around our code.

To run Cucumber tests from within IntelliJ, you will need to create a run configuration for Cucumber. This can be done using **Edit Configuration** from the **Run** menu tab. Then select Cucumber Java. Refer to the following image:

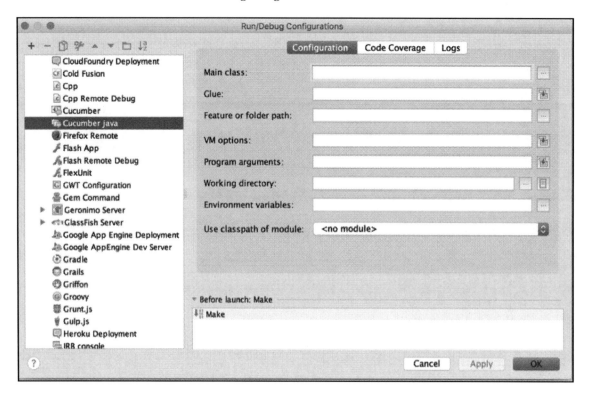

The changes to `BaseConversion` will look something like this:

```scala
package com.packt

  import scala.annotation.tailrec

  object BaseConversion {


    val hexTable =
      Array('0','1','2','3','4','5','6','7',
        '8','9','A','B','C','D','E','F')

    def decimalToHexadecimal(decimal: Number): Hexadecimal = {
      Hexadecimal(toHexadecimal(BigInt(decimal.number), "").toString)
    }


    def binaryToDecimal(binary: Number): Decimal = {
      val seq = binary.number.reverse.zipWithIndex.map { case (a, i) =>
        a.toString.toInt * math.pow(2, i) }
      Decimal(seq.sum.toInt.toString)
    }

    def hexadecimalToBinary(hexadecimal: Number): Decimal = {
      val seq = hexadecimal.number.reverse.zipWithIndex.map { case (a, i) =>
        hexTable.indexOf(a) * math.pow(16, i) }
      Decimal(seq.sum.toInt.toString)
    }

    def decimalToBinary(decimal: Number) = {
      Binary(toBinary(BigInt(decimal.number), "").toString)
    }

    @tailrec
    private def toBinary(num: BigInt, acc: String): String = {
      if (num < 2) (num.toInt + acc)
      else toBinary(num / 2, (num mod 2).toString ++ acc)
    }

    @tailrec
    private def toHexadecimal(num: BigInt, acc: String): String = {
      if (num < 16) (hexTable(num.toInt).toString + acc)
      else toHexadecimal(num / 16, hexTable((num mod 16).toInt).toString ++
acc)
    }
  }
```

Summary

In this chapter, we have discussed more approaches to testing. We have purposefully delved deeper into BDD. BDD is increasingly becoming an industry-wide accepted standard. This is due to the fact that there is a very high involvement of the customer and business, or its representation is omnipresent during the development process. The likelihood of developing something that is archaic or superfluous is low in this case.

6

Mock Objects and Stubs

Mocks and stubs are essential to any test-driven or behavior-driven testing frameworks:

> *"The term 'Mock Objects' has become a popular one to describe special case objects that mimic real objects for testing. Most language environments now have frameworks that make it easy to create mock objects. What's often not realized, however, is that mock objects are but one form of special case test object, one that enables a different style of testing."*

> *– Martin Fowler*

In this chapter, we will discuss:

- History of mock objects
- Couplings
- Stubs
- Mocks
- Fakes
- Spy
- Mocking frameworks

History

During one of my several Agile incarnations, I had the opportunity to work with Tim Mackinnon who was involved in the development of the concept of mock objects. I don't want to infringe on his rights to tell the story himself, which he had told me during our little gig together. In a nutshell, it was thought up at a brainstorming session between some members of a London-based architecture group. They had discussed the antipattern of having to introduce getters into their classes to make them testable. This was in the very early stages of Agile (1999) and terms like "scrum" and "Extreme Programming" hadn't been coined yet.

 There is a very interesting read at `http://www.mockobjects.com/2009/0` `9/brief-history-of-mock-objects.html`.

Since then there has been a constant love-hate relationship between developers who like mock objects and can swear by their experiences of their usage and developers who think mocking is, well let's just say, not the best thing to use with Scala. A very good example of this conundrum can be found at `https://www.reddit.com/r/programming/comments/9pk` `u9/mock_objects_and_dependency_injection_are_just/`.

Coupling

In software parlance, **coupling** refers to the gradation of interdependence between different modules. It measures how much impact does a change in one routine have in another. We can broadly distinguish between two major types of coupling: tight coupling and loose coupling. Two modules are considered tightly coupled if you cannot change one module without having a cascading effect on the second module. On the contrary, if one module can change resulting in little or no change in the other module, they are considered loosely coupled.

Coupling plays a major role in testability of your code. The more loosely coupled your code is, the more testable it is. It is not always easy to reduce or eliminate coupling, but since the introduction of dependency injection, it has become easier to test a module in isolation.

Dependency injection, also known as **Inversion of Control (IoC),** is a design pattern in which a dependency object (for example, a service) is passed in as a dependency to the dependant object (for example, a client). This is contrary to the traditional composition where the client would tell which service it would use. Instead, the client is injected with a service it should use.

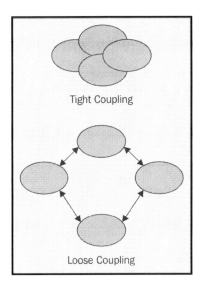

Even with loose coupling, we face the situation where to test class *A* that is loosely coupled with class *B* and *C*, we may have to create instances of class *B* and *C*. This gap is filled very nicely with mock objects and stubs.

Stubs

A **stub** is an object that yields predefined results based on a predetermined set of inputs. A stub is very restrictive in its usage. If we create a stub that will return "Land Rover Discovery Sports" whenever we call it with string "CK65ZSR", then it will be restricted to only this operation. If we call it with some other string, it wouldn't know what to do. In this case, depending on our implementation of the stub, it may throw an error or return null (or Scala's equivalent of null). There may be a bit of astuteness in the stub so it can remember how many times it has been called and with what parameters. This is done so that we can verify the behavior of the stub.

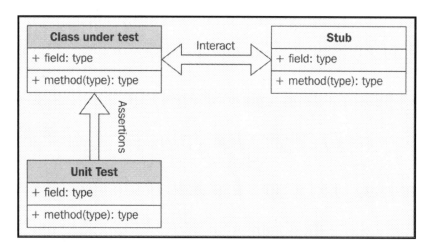

Mock objects

A **mock** is a stub on steroids. It is a stub and much more. Like a stub, a mock object also returns values that are premeditated. Apart from this, a mock object can also be programmed with expectations about the number of times the mock is called and in what order it is invoked. The use of mock objects leads to tests that test specific details about the interaction between the classes without the use of the actual class.

Expectations

Expectations are set on mock objects to define their behavior. Expectations are also a way of asserting that the class under test is working as expected. Exceptions can set expected responses, sequences in which methods should be called, or any errors that were expected. In general, the expectations just set the behavior of the mock object. It does not result in a test failure if one or more expectations are not invoked.

Example: If I have set my mock object with the expectation that it will be called three times and if my test only calls it one time, it will not result in a failure.

Verifications

Verifications on mock objects are set to verify that the expectations are met. This is to make sure that the expectations have been invoked as expected. Verification of expectations complete the testing cycle in the sense that we have set an expectation on a mock object to behave in a certain manner, and once the test is finished we verify that the mock object did actually behave in the expected manner.

If we continue from the example about expectations, if we then verify our expectation that the mock object has indeed been called three times, my test would fail. This is because the test only invoked the mock object once.

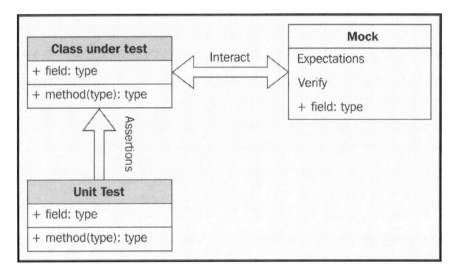

Fakes

Fake objects are working implementations of the interface or trait. This implementation is not production-like but instead takes a shortcut. Therefore, a fake object is just confined to the test harness and does not make it to the production code.

Fakes are dumb implementations and do not have any concept of expectations and verifications. Fakes arise from the school of thought that the interaction of the behavior of the dependency should not be a matter of concern for a test that is concentrating on testing the client.

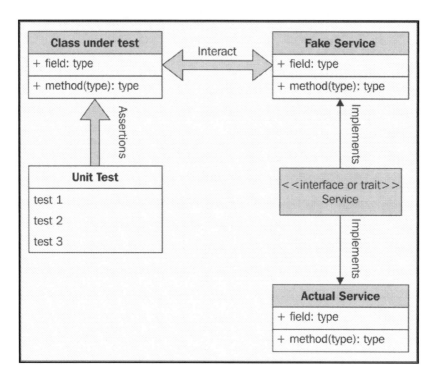

Spy

A spy differs from mock objects in term of behavior corroboration. A spy acts more like a logger and instead of setting up behavioral expectations, it will log the calls made to the co-worker. A unit test will later assert the logs from the spy.

Mocking frameworks

We will only confine our study to the list of mocking frameworks that are compatible with Scala. There will be similar frameworks or bridge APIs to the same frameworks available for unit testing other languages.

JMock

As the name suggests, JMock was originally written for test-driven development of Java code by providing support for mock objects and stubs. Given that Scala runs on JVM and can use Java classes, it is quite easy to start using JMock when test-driving Scala code.

Moreover, it is also easier for developers who have used JMock with Java to make a transition into writing test-driven Scala code.

Advantages of JMock

The following are JMock advantages:

- Easier to make a transition from Java to Scala
- Quite easy to set up and use
- Support for annotations becomes less obtrusive
- Ability to define precise interactions between objects
- Most new IDEs have support/plugins for JMock and can code assist in auto-completion.
- Easily plugs into ScalaTest or Specs2
- Extensible

ScalaTest has a `JMockCycle` class, which encapsulates the life cycle of a JMock Mockery (`org.jmock.Mockery`) object. JMockCycle provides some syntactic sugar to enable retrofitting JMock for use with Scala.

If you were using JMock for Java, you would normally create a `Mockery` context object like this:

```
val context = new Mockery
context.setImposteriser(ClassImposteriser.INSTANCE)
```

The Scala equivalent of this, encapsulated under JMockCycle, looks something like this:

```
val cycle = new JMockCycle
import cycle._
val mockCollaborator = mock[Collaborator]
```

A typical test using JMockCycle will look like this:

```
val cycle = new JMockCycle
import cycle._
```

```
val mockCollaborator = mock[Collaborator]

expecting { e => import e._
  oneOf (mockCollaborator).addToTotal(200)
  exactly(3).of (mockCollaborator).addedToTotal(200)
}

whenExecuting {
  classUnderTest.addToTotal(200)
  classUnderTest.addToTotal(200)
  classUnderTest.addToTotal(200)
}
```

The expecting method creates a new instance of Expectations and passes it to the function you provide that will set the expectations. When the function returns, the returned Expectations object is sent to Mockery's checking method.

whenExecuting will execute the functions passed to it and then will invoke asserIsSatisfied on the Mockery context object for verification.

 Please visit http://www.jmock.org/ for more information about jMock.

EasyMock

EasyMock, as the name suggests, makes mocking much more expedient by dynamically creating mock objects. EasyMock uses a Java proxy mechanism to dynamically generate mock objects. Similar to JMock, EasyMock was originally written for test-driving Java code. ScalaTest provides the EasyMockSugar trait that adds basic syntactic sugar that enables the use of EasyMock for test-driving Scala code.

A typical test with EasyMock will look like this:

```
val mockCollaborator = mock[Collaborator]

expecting {
  mockCollaborator.documentAdded("Document")
  mockCollaborator.documentChanged("Document")
  lastCall.times(3)
}

whenExecuting(mockCollaborator) {
```

```
    classUnderTest.addDocument("Document", new Array[Byte](0))
    classUnderTest.addDocument("Document", new Array[Byte](0))
    classUnderTest.addDocument("Document", new Array[Byte](0))
    classUnderTest.addDocument("Document", new Array[Byte](0))
}
```

Here, `whenExecuting` passes `mockCollaborator` to `replay` to execute the code that uses the mock, and to `verify` to the mock. `whenExecuting` also allows multiple mocks to be passed to it.

The optional `expecting` clause depicts which statements are setting expectations on the mock. `replay` indicates that you are finished setting up the mock and are ready to use it.

 Please visit `http://easymock.org/` to learn more about EasyMock.

Mockito

MockitoSugar in ScalaTest provides syntactic sugar for using Mockito with ScalaTest.

In my experience, I have found Mockito to be the easiest to use among all the frameworks. It is quite easy to create a mock from `ServiceClass` by simply using `mock[ServiceClass]`.

Mockito leads to a very understandable test format. I think that is one of the reasons for its popularity over jMock and EasyMock.

Let us rewrite the same example from jMock and EasyMock with Mockito. It will look something like this:

```
// First, create the mock object
val mockService = mock[ServiceClass]

// Create the class under test and pass the mock to it
classUnderTest = new ClassUnderTest
classUnderTest.addService(mock)

// Use the class under test
classUnderTest.createPayroll("Person1", 1000)
classUnderTest.createPayroll("Person1", 4000)
classUnderTest.createPayroll("Person1", 6000)
classUnderTest.createPayroll("Person1", 19000)
```

```
// Then verify the class under test used the
// mock object as expected
verify(mockCollaborator).createInitalPayroll("Person1")
verify(mockCollaborator, times(3)).changePayroll("Person1")
```

ScalaMock

ScalaMock was perhaps the first mocking framework which understood that Scala is a different language than Java. It played on the fact that Scala allows both functional and object-oriented code. Therefore, the mocking framework for Scala needs to be able to mock both these as aspects of a Scala class.

It is a native framework and it allows mocking of both functions and objects. Paul Butcher wrote Scala mock.

Advantages of ScalaMock

- Type safe
- Open source
- Support for Scala-specific features such as:
    - Operator methods
    - Method overloading
    - Pattern matching
    - Parameterized methods
- Compatible with both ScalaTest and Specs2

We need to mix `MockFactory` into our test suite for us to be able to use `ScalaMock` with `ScalaTest`, as per the following example:

```
import org.scalatest.FlatSpec
import org.scalamock.scalatest.MockFactory

class BaseSuite extends FlatSpec with MockFactory with ...
```

mockFunction

Functions can be mocked using `mockFuntion`, as per the following example:

```
//Creates mock function which expects single Int parameters
// and returns a String

val m = mockFunction[Int, String]

//Then we set expectation on this mock that it is called once
//with parameter 86 and it returns "Eighty Six"

m expects (86) returning "Eighty Six" once
```

Proxy mocks

A proxy mock is used to mock Scala traits or Java interfaces. The mixin `ProxyMockFactory` in our test suite can create proxy mocks:

```
val house = mock[Building]
house expects 'setNumberOfWindows withArgs (5)
house expects 'setNumberOfDoors withArgs (2)

house expects 'openDoor once
```

Here we create a proxy mock house and set expectations on the method calls during our test.

Generated mocks

Generated mocks are used to mock Scala classes. To do this, they make use of the ScalaMock compiler plugin. Generated classes can be mocked using the `org.scalamock.annotation.mock` annotation. You can also mock a class and its companion object using the `org.scalamock.annotation.mockWithCompanion` annotation. Similarly, singleton objects can be mocked using the `org.scalamock.annotation.mockObject` annotation.

Let's dig a little deeper

ScalaMock is worth exploring in more detail as part of this book per se concentrates on TDD with Scala.

Specifying expectations

As with other mocking frameworks, ScalaMock allows expectations to be set in the arguments with which the function will be called. This can be done using `withArgs` or `withArguments`.

Specifying the argument is not necessary, and if no argument is specified then the mock will accept any number and type of arguments.

The value of the argument can be specified as literals, epsilons (for floating point numbers), or wild cards, as per the following example:

```
house expects ("Knocks", 2)
house expects ("Residents", *)
house expects ("Rent", ~1526)
```

Repeated parameters can be mocked in expectations using `**`:

```
m expects 'takesRepeatedParameter withArgs
(42, **("red", "green", "blue"))
```

Mocks can also be set to return values:

```
calc expects (2, 4) returning 6
```

Mocks can also be set to throw exceptions:

```
calc expects (0, 2) throws new AirthmeticException("Divide by zero")
```

Summary

There is a love-hate relationship between developers and mock objects. On the one hand, there are obvious benefits of being able to test classes in isolation. This also evolves into a more loosely coupled architecture and there is greater reusability of code.

On other hand, mocks couple the test code to the actual implementation of the class being tested. If the test code undergoes some major refactoring, it might result in changes in the expectations and verifications of the mocks in the test. This deviates from the principle of the segregation of test and application code.

A mocking framework is a great tool in your development arsenal if rightly used. There is definitely such a thing as too much mocking, so steer clear away from it.

7
Property-Based Testing

Sometimes, to make our tests exhaustive, we need to test against as many of the test cases as possible. Writing a test for each testable input obviously cannot be the answer. Property-based testing framework executes the same test over and over with generated input. This can easily be contrasted with the traditional example-based testing, which has a unit test depicting a sample scenario with test data that is descriptive of that scenario. This chapter will cover the following topics:

- Property-based testing
- Table-driven property checks
- Generator-driven property checks
- ScalaCheck

Introduction to property-based testing

In modern software development gauge, tests are the measure of the quality of your software. It is more than imperative to continually write good tests. The definition of a good test may change from developer to developer and from project to project. It is also dependant on the type of technology used, as some have extensive frameworks to help unit testing, whereas some are very rigid and/or have a smaller selection of frameworks to support unit testing.

I cannot stress enough how much the amount of test coverage of the application code builds up developers and other stakeholder's confidence in the application. I have witnessed systems that have succumbed under their own weight of over complication, the wrong choice of technologies, and a lack of unit tests.

Writing tests is not easy work. There is lot to consider while writing a test, such as the test data to use, its coverage, and edge cases. This can result in huge number of tests. Alternatively, we can use property-based tested to test the behavior with a large range of inputs.

The quality of the software is dependant on the quality of the tests. The better the tests, the higher the software quality. From the developer's perspective, it also means that it is tremendously hard to write good tests. For example, even to write a trivial unit test, the developer needs to consider the end use of the application code, possible edge cases in the bounds of allowed input and how the application should react to unexpected behavior. All this leads to a huge number of possible test scenarios, which need to be tested for the testing to be exhaustive.

Property-based testing ensures that a property is tested to hold true to an assortment of inputs. Property in this instance is an elevated explanation of a behavior. It can be contrasted with the traditional test approach where the test would only test the behavior based on a few (three or four) data points. Property-based testing uses a range of input data points for which the property should hold true.

The range of input to for property-based testing can be supplied through a table or it can be generated.

Table-driven properties

If there is a finite range of properties that would need to be tested, we can create a table of inputs. These inputs can then drive the tests by providing single row as input for each test run.

Table-driven tests are useful when there is a definitive range of values that you would want the test to run against. The benefit is that since the inputs/test values are not randomly generated the tests are always run against the same values from the table. It also makes the values visible to the reader of the test and facilitates the documentation purpose of the test.

We need to mix in the `TableDrivenPropertyChecks` trait for us to be able to write table-driven property tests.

This trait has one `forAll` method for each `TableForN` class (`TableFor1` through `TableFor22`). This method allows the property to be verified against each row of the table. This can be made conditional using the `wherever` clause.

We can rewrite all the tests in our example application to table-driven property tests:

BinaryToDecimalSpec:

```
package com.packt
import org.scalatest.prop.TableDrivenPropertyChecks
class BinaryToDecimalSpec extends UnitSpec with
TableDrivenPropertyChecks {
  it should "convert binary to decimal" in {
    val validCombos = Table(
        ("binary",   "decimal"),
        ("100100111101",   "2365"),
        ("111100011111110111",   "123895"),
        ("100000000000001110000001",   "8389505"),
        ("101111010101011101001101",   "3102541")
    )
    forAll(validCombos) { (binString:String, decString:String) =>
       var decimal = BaseConversion.binaryToDecimal(Binary(binString))
         decimal.number shouldBe decString
    }
  }
}
```

DecimalToBinarySpec:

```
package com.packt

import org.scalatest.prop.TableDrivenPropertyChecks

class DecimalBinarySpec extends UnitSpec with TableDrivenPropertyChecks {

  it should "convert decimal to binary" in {
    val validCombos =
      Table(
        ("binary",   "decimal"),
        ("100100111101", "2365"),
        ("111100011111110111", "123895"),
        ("100000000000001110000001", "8389505"),
        ("101111010101011101001101", "3102541")
    )
      forAll(validCombos) { (binString: String, decString: String) =>
      var binary = BaseConversion.decimalToBinary(Decimal(decString))
      binary.number shouldBe binString
    }
  }
}
```

DecimalToHexaDecimalSpec:

```
package com.packt

import org.scalatest.prop.TableDrivenPropertyChecks

class DecimalHexadecimalSpec extends UnitSpec with
TableDrivenPropertyChecks {


  it should "convert decimal to hex" in {
    val validCombos =
    Table(
      ("decimal",  "hexadecimal"),
      ("1243", "4DB"),
      ("11111122", "A98AD2"),
      ("2435255412343", "2370088A677"),
      ("8765432", "85BFF8")
    )
    forAll(validCombos) { (decStr: String, hexStr: String) =>
    var hex = BaseConversion.decimalToHexadecimal(Decimal(decStr))
    hex.number shouldBe hexStr
    }
  }
}
```

HexaDecimalToDecimalSpec:

```
com.packt

import org.scalatest.prop.TableDrivenPropertyChecks

class HexadecimalToDecimalSpec extends UnitSpec with
TableDrivenPropertyChecks {

  it should "convert hex to decimal" in {
    val validCombos =
    Table(
      ("decimal",  "hexadecimal"),
      ("171", "AB"),
      ("74667", "123AB"),
      ("11259375", "ABCDEF"),
    )
    forAll(validCombos) { (decString: String, hexString: String) =>
    var decimal =
BaseConversion.hexadecimalToDecimal(Hexadecimal(hexString))
    decimal.number shouldBe decString
    }
```

```
      }
  }
```

The overloaded forAll methods are used to test the property against the data from the table. The forAll method takes two parameters, table, and a function, whose arguments are compatible with the data in the rows of the table. It will also throw TableDrivenPropertyCheckExcepton if the function interrupts or fails. It will throw DiscardedEvalutationException if the test fails for any row. This exception is also thrown by the whenever clause if no row in the table matches the clause.

Table-driven property tests can be used for testing stateful function, such as a workflow or combination of invalid test cases.

Let's see what the output would look like for a failing test. In this case, we will modify one of the previous tests with an invalid value in the table to make it fail. This will also validate the usefulness of the test.

Modified BinaryToDecimalSpec:

```scala
package com.packt

import org.scalatest.prop.TableDrivenPropertyChecks

class BinaryToDecimalSpec extends UnitSpec
  with TableDrivenPropertyChecks {
  it should "convert binary to decimal" in {
    val validCombos =
      Table(
        ("binary",  "decimal"),
        ("100100111101",  "21365"),
        ("11110001111110111",  "123895"),
        ("1000000000000001110000001",  "838950x5"),
        ("1011110101011101001101",  "3102541")
      )

    forAll(validCombos) { (binString:String, decString:String) =>
      var decimal = BaseConversion.binaryToDecimal(Binary(binString))
      decimal.number shouldBe decString
    }
  }
}
```

When we run this test, the output will look something like this:

```
Done: 0 of 1  Failed: 1  (2.664 s)
/Library/Java/JavaVirtualMachines/jdk1.7.0_65.jdk/Contents/Home/bin/java ...
Testing started at 23:57 ...

TestFailedException was thrown during property evaluation. (BinaryToDecimalSpec.scala:16)
  Message: "2[]365" was not equal to "2[1]365"
  Location: (BinaryToDecimalSpec.scala:18)
  Occurred at table row 0 (zero based, not counting headings), which had values (
    binary = 100100111101,
    decimal = 21365
  )
ScalaTestFailureLocation: com.packt.BinaryToDecimalSpec$$anonfun$1 at (BinaryToDecimalSpec.scala:16)
org.scalatest.exceptions.TableDrivenPropertyCheckFailedException: TestFailedException was thrown during property evalu
  Message: "2[]365" was not equal to "2[1]365"
  Location: (BinaryToDecimalSpec.scala:18)
  Occurred at table row 0 (zero based, not counting headings), which had values (
    binary = 100100111101,
    decimal = 21365
  )
    at org.scalatest.prop.TableFor2$$anonfun$apply$7.apply(TableFor1.scala:399)
    at org.scalatest.prop.TableFor2$$anonfun$apply$7.apply(TableFor1.scala:390)
    at scala.collection.TraversableLike$WithFilter$$anonfun$foreach$1.apply(TraversableLike.scala:733)
    at scala.collection.mutable.ResizableArray$class.foreach(ResizableArray.scala:59)
    at scala.collection.mutable.ArrayBuffer.foreach(ArrayBuffer.scala:48)
    at scala.collection.TraversableLike$WithFilter.foreach(TraversableLike.scala:732)
    at org.scalatest.prop.TableFor2.apply(TableFor1.scala:390)
    at org.scalatest.prop.TableDrivenPropertyChecks$class.forAll(TableDrivenPropertyChecks.scala:396)
    at com.packt.BinaryToDecimalSpec.forAll(BinaryToDecimalSpec.scala:5)
    at com.packt.BinaryToDecimalSpec$$anonfun$1.apply$mcV$sp(BinaryToDecimalSpec.scala:16)
    at com.packt.BinaryToDecimalSpec$$anonfun$1.apply(BinaryToDecimalSpec.scala:6)
    at com.packt.BinaryToDecimalSpec$$anonfun$1.apply(BinaryToDecimalSpec.scala:6)
    at org.scalatest.Transformer$$anonfun$apply$1.apply$mcV$sp(Transformer.scala:22)
    at org.scalatest.OutcomeOf$class.outcomeOf(OutcomeOf.scala:85)
    at org.scalatest.OutcomeOf$.outcomeOf(OutcomeOf.scala:104)
    at org.scalatest.Transformer.apply(Transformer.scala:22)
    at org.scalatest.Transformer.apply(Transformer.scala:20)
    at org.scalatest.FlatSpecLike$$anon$1.apply(FlatSpecLike.scala:1647)
    at org.scalatest.Suite$class.withFixture(Suite.scala:1122)
    at org.scalatest.FlatSpec.withFixture(FlatSpec.scala:1683)
    at org.scalatest.FlatSpecLike$class.invokeWithFixture$1(FlatSpecLike.scala:1644)
    at org.scalatest.FlatSpecLike$$anonfun$runTest$1.apply(FlatSpecLike.scala:1656)
    at org.scalatest.FlatSpecLike$$anonfun$runTest$1.apply(FlatSpecLike.scala:1656)
    at org.scalatest.SuperEngine.runTestImpl(Engine.scala:306)
```

It can be seen from the output that the error message is quite descriptive. This helps understand why the test is breaking and what needs to be done to fix it.

Generator-driven properties

Sometimes, we want our properties to be checked against a randomly generated set of inputs. These input values are generated within some bounds that we can define with conditions. One example is, when we have a compression algorithm that needs testing. Instead of using a predefined list of strings, we can have a generated set of strings so that our function is tested against them.

Generator-driven property tests make use of ScalaCheck; therefore, make sure ScalaCheck JAR is included in the classpath. Your test will need to mixin `GeneratorDrivenPropertyCheck`. If your test uses both table-driven property checks and Generator-driven property checks, then mixin trait `PropertyChecks` as it extends both `TableDrivenPropertyChecks` and `GeneratorDrivenPropertyChecks`.

ScalaCheck

ScalaCheck libraries are used for Generator-driven, property-based testing. ScalaCheck can be used for testing both Java and Scala. ScalaCheck is written in Scala and was inspired by QuickCheck for Haskell.

It is quite easy to introduce ScalaCheck in you is test harness, as it only needs Scala to work with and is not dependent on any other external libraries.

To include ScalaCheck in your application test harness, add this line to your `build.sbt` file:
`libraryDependencies += "org.scalacheck" %% "scalacheck" % "1.13.0" % "test"`
For an in-depth view of ScalaCheck, check out, `http://www.artima.com/shop/scalacheck`.

Generators

ScalaCheck uses Generators for creating test data. Quite simply put, a **Generator** is a function that takes some parameters to generate some value. The generated value has a direct correlation to the generation parameters. Generators are represented by the `org.scalacheck.Gen` object. The `Gen` object provides many methods to create new Generators or modify the existing ones. It is pertinent to learn how to use the `Gen` class, so we are able to create test data that is required for testing our property.

Generators form the basics of ScalaCheck. `Gen[T]` can be seen as a function of type `Gen.Params => Option[T]`. This, though, is a very simplistic view of the `Gen` class. The `Gen` class provides much more like functionality to map Generators or running for-comprehensions on Generators. There are combinators inside the `Gen` object that can be used to modify the behavior of the Generator. These combinators are part of the `org.scalacheck.Gen` module and can be combined using for-comprehension.

Let's look at a simple Generator that will generate two strings, where the second string is always double the first one:

```
val strings = (for {
   s1 <- Gen.alphaStr
   s2 <- Gen.alphaStr
 } yield (s1, s2)).suchThat( m => m._2.length > m._1.length * 2  )
```

Here, we used the `alphaStr` combinator from the `Gen` object to generate two random strings, and then we tie the results together with the `suchThat` clause by mandating that the length of the second string should be greater than double the length of first one.

We have also used the for-comprehension to combine the two Generators together so that a tuple of two strings is generated.

We can also create a Generator that chooses one of a given distribution:

```
val vowel = Gen.oneOf('A', 'E', 'I', 'O', 'U', 'Y')
```

The distribution of the `oneOf` clause is uniform by default, but it can be controlled using frequency combinatory:

```
val vowel = Gen.frequency(
   (3, 'A'),
   (4, 'E'),
   (2, 'I'),
   (3, 'O'),
   (1, 'U'),
   (1, 'Y')
)
```

This means that `'E'` will be returned four times more than `'U'`.

Generating case classes

Generators can also be used to generate Case Classes, for example:

```
val epayeOrders: Arbitrary[EPayeOrder] = Arbitrary((for {
   districtNumber <- Gen.containerOfN(3, Gen.numChar)
   checkCharater <- Gen.alphaChar
   registerNumber <- Gen.containerOfN(6, Gen.numChar)
   registerAlphaNum <- Gen.containerOfN(2, Gen.alphaNumChar)
   month <- Gen.chooseNum(1, 12)
```

```
year <- Gen.chooseNum(10, 99)
  } yield EPayeOrder (
    Seq.empty[Char] ++
    districtNumber ++
    Seq('P', checkCharater) ++
    registerNumber ++
    registerAlphaNum ++ year.toString.toCharArray ++
      StringUtils.leftPad(month.toString, 2, '0').toCharArray)
    .mkString.toUpperCase)
    .suchThat(_.length == 17)
)
```

Here, `EPayeOrder` is a case class. The Generator in example combines the results from various combinators using for-comprehension, to create an instance of `EPayeOrder`.

Conditional Generators

We can also add conditions to the Generators. We have already seen examples of this using the `suchThat` clause. Another example is as follows:

```
val primes = for {
  s1 <- Gen.chooseNum(10, 100).suchThat(n => !((2 until n/2)
  exists(n%_==0)))
} yield s1
```

In this example, we generate prime numbers between given range.

Generating containers

Generators combinators such as `containerOf`, `nonEmptyContainerOf`, and `containerOfN` can also be used to generate sequences, for example:

```
val genIntList = Gen.containerOf[List,Int](Gen.oneOf(4, 6, 7))
```

It supports list, array, stream, set, and ArrayList.

Arbitrary Generator

ScalaCheck also provides a unique Generator, `org.scalacheck.Arbitrary.arbitrary`, that is used to generate arbitrary values of any type, for example:

```
val string = Arbitrary.arbitrary[String] suchThat (_.length > 10)
```

This generates an arbitrary string of length greater than 10.

Generation statistics

We can also collate data about the generation process to verify the distribution of randomness. This statistical data can be used to check whether all the test cases are being run or whether we are missing some edge cases. This can be done using `Prop.classify` or `Prop.collect`:

```
import org.scalacheck.Prop._

val prop1 = forAll { l: Seq[String] =>
  classify(ordered(l), "sorted") {
    classify(l.length > 5, "long", "tiny") {
      l.reverse.reverse == l
    }
  }
}
```

The output will look something like this:

```
scala> prop1.check
+ OK, passed 100 tests.
> Collected test data:
78% long
16% tiny, sorted
6% tiny
```

Here, we can see that the distribution is not uniform and there is no test case for the sorted long list. Therefore, we may have to write our own Generator to cover this condition.

Executing property checks

The simplest way to execute property-based tests is to call the `check` method on the on the property. We have seen this in the last example from the previous section. This method has the following signature:

```
def check(params: Test.Parameters, p: Prop): Test.Result
```

ScalaCheck has a `Test` module that is responsible for test execution. This module executes the test with increasing test data. It also determines that if there is no failure after a certain number of checks then the test is passed.

The `Test.Parameters` trait is used to manipulate the size of test data, number of executions, and retries for argument generation failure.

The `Test.Result` trait encapsulates the result and some statistics from the test run. The most frequently used property inside this trait is `status`, which is of type `Test.Status`. It can have one of these values:

```
case object Passed extends Status

sealed case class Proved(args: List[Arg]) extends Status

sealed case class Failed(args: List[Arg], label: String) extends Status

case object Exhausted extends Status

sealed case class PropException(args: List[Arg], e: Throwable, label:
String) extends Status

sealed case class GenException(e: Throwable) extends Status
```

Our own Generator-driven property checks

It's hands-on time once again. Let's create some Generator-driven property checks for our example application. We will write two tests. The first one will generate decimals, convert then to binary, and then re-covert the binary to decimal to verify that our decimal to binary and binary to decimal conversion is idempotent. Then, we will do same to test decimal to hexadecimal and vice versa conversions.

DecimalToBinaryGenSpec:

```
package com.packt

import org.scalatest.prop.{GeneratorDrivenPropertyChecks}
import org.scalacheck.Gen
import scala.collection.JavaConversions._

class DecimalToBinaryGenSpec extends UnitSpec with
GeneratorDrivenPropertyChecks {
  it should "convert decimal to binary and back to decimal" in {
    val decimals = (for {
      c1 <- Gen.chooseNum(2,100000)
      } yield c1.toString).suchThat(_ != "")

    forAll(decimals){ (decimalStr:String) =>
```

```
        var binary = BaseConversion.decimalToBinary(Decimal(decimalStr))
        var decimal = BaseConversion.binaryToDecimal(binary)
        decimal.number shouldBe decimalStr
      }
    }
  }
```

You may see the following error (or similar), while compiling this test:

```
Error:(13, 21) type mismatch;
found : (org.scalacheck.Gen[A],
DecimalToBinaryGenSpec.this.PropertyCheckConfigParam*)
required: ?C[?E]
Note that implicit conversions are not applicable because they are
ambiguous:
both method ArrowAssoc in object Predef of type [A](self: A)ArrowAssoc[A]
and method Ensuring in object Predef of type [A](self: A)Ensuring[A]
are possible conversion functions from (org.scalacheck.Gen[A],
DecimalToBinaryGenSpec.this.PropertyCheckConfigParam*) to ?C[?E]
forAll(decimals){ (decimalStr:String) =>
^
```

This is because of the `Inspectors` trait, which is mixin with `UnitSpec`. You can remove `Inspectors` trait from `UnitSpec` to get this test compiling. Your `UnitSpec` should look something like this:

```
package com.packt
import org.scalatest._
abstract class UnitSpec extends FlatSpec
                          with Matchers
                          with OptionValues
                          with Inside
```

DecimalToHexadecimalGenSpec:

```
package com.packt

import org.scalacheck.Gen
import org.scalatest.prop.GeneratorDrivenPropertyChecks

class DecimalToHexadecimalGenSpec extends UnitSpec with
GeneratorDrivenPropertyChecks {
  it should "convert decimal to hexadecimal and back to decimal" in {
    val decimals = (for {
      c1 <- Gen.chooseNum(2,100000)
    } yield c1.toString).suchThat(_ != "")

    forAll(decimals){ (decimalStr:String) =>
```

```
      var hex = BaseConversion.decimalToHexadecimal(Decimal(decimalStr))
      var decimal = BaseConversion.hexadecimalToDecimal(hex)
      decimal.number shouldBe decimalStr
      }
   }
}
```

Summary

It must have been evident from this chapter how useful property-based testing is to remove redundant tests and have maximum coverage. Both, table-driven and Generator-driven property checks have their own niche. They also have some downsides, as the test data is not well documented, especially when Generator-driven checks are used to test properties. They can be clubbed with more detailed examples or BDD instructions, which provide for the documentation aspect.

8
Scala TDD with Specs2

Specs2 is another popular library, which is used to write an executable specification for Scala. Specs2 is contrarily focused than ScalaTest. It also has a different perspective. It is another arsenal in your gambit of writing tests for Scala code. In this chapter, we will look at:

- Introduction to Specs2
- Differences between Specs2 and ScalaTest
- Setting up Specs2
- Unit specification
- Functional specification
- Matchers

Introduction to Specs2

Much like ScalaTest, Specs2 also works with SBT. There are both similarities and differences between Specs2 and ScalaTest. Some unique differences between Specs2 and ScalaTest give the developer choice of one over the other depending on the functionality required.

 There is a very interesting presentation about Specs2 at `https://www.parl eys.com/tutorial/514892260364bc17fc56bde3/chapter0/about`.

Differences between Specs2 and ScalaTest

The main differences between ScalaTest and Specs2 are:

- The overall structure of the test in Specs2 is different to that in ScalaTest.
- Specs2 has a different set of Matchers with different syntax.
- Specs2 tests are primarily dedicated to **behavior-driven development (BDD)**, whereas ScalaTest tests are more generic.
- ScalaTest provides much more choice and versatility. For example, to write BDD-like Specs2 in ScalaTest, one can use `Spec`, `FeatureSpec`, `WordSpec`, `FlatSpec`, and `GivenWhenThen` traits along with `ShouldMatchers` or `MustMatcher`. This gives the developer more flexibility to follow his/her own style of writing specifications.
- Specs2 has a significantly higher number of Matchers than ScalaTest. Most of them are for a particular need. For example, in Specs2, you can say:

  ```
  aFile mustBe aDirectory
  ```

- Where Specs2 has individual Matchers for `java.io.Files`, ScalaTest does not have similar Matchers.
- Another difference between ScalaTest and Spec is implicit conversions. ScalaTest only has one implicit conversion, which we achieve using the `===` operator. This can, however, be turned off in ScalaTest using a single line of code. This is the only implicit conversion get for free in ScalaTest. There are other implicit conversions, which can be used by mixin other traits. Contrary to this Specs2 gives you dozens of implicit conversion just by extending the `Specification` class. In practice, this doesn't make much of a difference. The only difference would be that the test code would be more readable without explicit conversions.
- Specs2 has a bigger collection of operators than the basic five operators, which come packaged with ScalaTest. It only define these basic operators:

  ```
  ===
  ```

  ```
  >
  ```

  ```
  <
  ```

  ```
  >=
  ```

  ```
  <=
  ```

- In Specs2, other than the basic operators, you can also find operators like:

```
->-

>>

|

|>

!

^^^
```

All these have a special meaning in Specs2.

- Specs2 has data tables. This allows the use of number of examples, which can drive the test, much like property-driven tests.
- Specs2 tests differ from ScalaTest as they can be concurrently executed in a separate thread.

At the end of the day, both Specs2 and ScalaTest are able to achieve pretty much the same thing, sometime in their vanilla form or other time by mixing some helper traits. The use of one over another is a matter of preference.

Setting up Specs2

The following dependencies and resolvers need to be added to `build.sbt` to set up Specs2 so that it can run from SBT:

```
version := "1.0.0"
name := "Specs2 Setup"

libraryDependencies += "org.specs2" %% "specs2-core" % "3.8.4" % "test"

scalacOptions in Test ++= Seq("-Yrangepos")
```

We can provide a sequence of Maven repositories for SBT to use for resolving dependencies using `resolvers`.

Styles

A specification would normally include two things:

- Informal text describing the functionality of the application code under test.
- Scala code describing the inputs to the test and then comparing the output with the expected output.

Specs2 provides two ways of doing this:

- We can write all the informal text in one place and all the Scala code somewhere else. This style of specification is referred to as "acceptance" specification. We will discuss this in more detail later. Since the text is in one place, it is much easier for a non-developer to read the test and endorse the specification.
- Alternatively, the Scala code and the text can be interleaved with each other. This structure is more akin to the traditional unit test framework like xUnit. This is called **unit specification**.

There are pros and cons of using both styles.

Acceptance specifications are simpler to read as a story but necessitate constant switching between the text and the code. You also must write an `is` method, which holds the body of the test.

It is easier to navigate unit specifications, as the text tends to be lost in a sea of code.

Let's look at these styles in more detail.

Unit specifications

This first test we will look at is similar in its purpose to a ScalaTest. The only difference is in its layout and strategy:

```scala
import org.specs2.mutable._
import org.joda.time.Period

class FootballTeamsUnitSpec extends Specification {
  "A Football Team" should {

  """have a getGoalKeeper function which
  selects the plater who has been earmarked to be the goalkeeper""" in {

    val firstTeam = new FootballTeam("Gaurav's Team", 2016,
```

```
        Some(List(new Player("Tom", "Midfielder"),
            new Player("Freddy", "Midfielder"),
            new Player("Steve", "Center Forward"),
            new Player("Dale", "Goal Keeper"),))
    )

    firstTeam.getGoalkeeper.get.name must be_==("Dale")
      }
    }
  }
```

A unit specification will normally start with a string that would describe the application code we would be testing. This is followed by `should`. This would look very similar to ScalaTest. The block that follows has one or more test description that is in turn followed by block of actual test code.

Unit specification extends `org.spec2.mutable.Specification`.

It is evident from the example that Specs2 has different Matchers than ScalaTest. For example, we used `must be_==` instead of `must be (...)`.

As mentioned earlier, Specs2 tests run asynchronously and independent of each other in separate threads using Promise. **Promises** are Scala processes that make use of Actor model and run in individual threads. These threads can send objects, `ExecutedResult` in this case, to each other. This in turn is used to send the result of the test back.

The resultant application code is driven by the test:

```
class FootballTeam private (val teamName, val players:Option[List[Player]])
{

  def getGoalkeeper:Player {
        players.getOrElse.filter(_.position="Goal Keeper")
  }
}
```

Another way to write a unit specification in Specs2 is using >>:

```
class AnotherTest extends org.specs2.mutable.Specification {
  "this is another specification" >> {
    "where first example must be true" >> {
      "Hello" must_== "Hello"
    }
    "where second specification must be false" >> {
      "World" must_!= "Earth"
    }
  }
```

```
}
```

The >> blocks can be nested, and this permits you to construct your tests so that the outmost blocks define a broad-spectrum situation while the deepest ones define more precise perspectives.

Acceptance specification

Acceptance specification is distinguished from unit specification by separating the test code from the expectation definition. Let's look at another example of how to use acceptance specification in Specs2:

```
package com.packt

import org.specs2.Specification

class ExampleAcceptanceSpec extends Specification { def is =
  "Our example specification"              ^
      "and we should run t1 here"               ! t1 ^
      "and we should run t2 here"   ! t2

   def t1 = success
   def t2 = pending
}
```

The thing not to be missed here is the specification that is imported. Unlike the unit specification, we are importing org.spec2.Specification here instead of org.spec2.mutable.Specification.

In this example, the is method is the one that bootstraps the entire test. A fragment, which contains all the examples, is returned in this method.

The technique gives back a Fragments object containing every one of the cases. There are two individual strategies inside ExampleAcceptanceSpec. The first one will run the approach t1, as specified after the primer string. Then, after the second introductory string, we specify t2 as the strategy to be run. We use the ! operator for the purpose of separating the test into blocks, which can be run in individual threads.

Carets separate the tests. Any string that does not use the ! operator to call a method is viewed as a header for the next tests. In the preceding example, it is a simple specification that is followed by a ^. The carets separate the details. There is no caret following the last line as no division is required.

Since the Scala Actor model is used for running Specs2 tests, SBT will run the test and collate the results to be reported:

```
[info] Compiling 1 Scala source to /home/packt/scala_tdd_book.git
/chapter8/target/scala-2.9.2/test-classes...
[info] Our example specification
[info] + and we should run t1 here
[info] * and we should run t2 here PENDING
[info]
[info] Total for specification ExampleAcceptanceSpec
[success] Total time: 5 s
```

The default behavior of Specs2 to run the tests in parallel can be switched off if needed to make the run tests sequentially. This can be done by adding `args(sequential=true)` to the test, for example:

```
class ExampleSequentialAcceptanceSpec extends Specification { def is =
  args(sequential = true)                     ^
  "This is an example specification"        ^
     "and this should run t1"            ! t1 ^
     "and this example should run t2"    ! t2

  def t1 = success
  def t2 = pending
}
```

In the preceding specification results, the + indicates that and this should run `f1 ran` successfully. The last test result shown next to PENDING bears a * symbol to state that the test is pending. Note that this is a simple specification and has no preceding symbol, because the line never invoked an Actor with `!`. It is just considered informational, much like the way informers are used in ScalaTest.

We'll create an `Employee` test that will add a middle name to an employee and has a `fullName` method to get the full name of the employee. The general target is to ascertain that an `Employee` object can optionally include a middle name:

```
package com.packt.chapter8

import org.specs2.Specification

class EmployeeAcceptanceSpec extends Specification { def is =
  "An employee should have a middle name at construction"                  ^
     """An employee should be able to be constructed with a middle
     name and get it back calling 'middleName'""" !
     makeAnEmployeeWithMiddleName   ^
     """An employee should be able to have a full name made of the first
```

```
                and last name
           given a first and last name at construction time""" !
              testFullNameWithFirstAndLast
     """An employee should be able to have a full name made of the first,
          middle and last name
            given a first, middle, and last name at construction time""" !
                testFullNameWithFirstMiddleAndLast

     def makeAnEmployeeWithMiddleName = pending
     def testFullNameWithFirstAndLast = pending
     def testFullNameWithFirstMiddleAndLast = pending
}
```

In this acceptance test, there are three specifications. This topic is supported by three test specifications. All three are pending for now.

At this point, we will replace the pending specifications with some useful tests:

```
package com.packt.chapter8
import org.specs2.Specification

class EmployeeAcceptanceSpec extends Specification { def is =
  "An employee should have a middle name"                          ^
     """An employee should be able to be constructed with a Option[String]
        middle name and
        we should be able to get it back calling 'middleName'""" !
        makeAnEmployeeWithMiddleName ^
     """An employee should be able to have a full name made of the first
     and last name
        given a first and last name at construction time"""
              ! testFullNameWithFirstAndLast

     """An employee should be able to have a full name
     made of the first, middle and last name where first, middle,
     and last name at construction time"""
                ! testFullNameWithFirstMiddleAndLast


     def makeAnEmployeeWithMiddleName = {
       val gaurav = new Employee("Gaurav", "Maken", "Sood")
       gaurav.middleName must be_==(Some("Maken"))
     }

     def testFullNameWithFirstAndLast = {
       val khush = new Employee("Khushboo", "Sood")
       khush.fullName should be_==("Khushboo Sood")
     }
```

```
def testFullNameWithFirstMiddleAndLast = {
  val kids = new Employee("Johan", "And", "Johan")
  kids.fullName should be_==("Johan And Johan")
}
}
```

Matchers

Just like ScalaTest, the Matchers in Specs2 serve the purpose of verifying the results against the expectations. The results of the tests are compared with some expected values, and this is done using Matchers. This is the classic **arrange-act-assert** archetype.

The most simple example would be a specification for an object that returns the full name of an employee:

```
// describe the functionality
s2"the getFullName method should return full name of the employee $e1"

// give an example with some code
def e1 = Employee.getFullName() must beEqualTo("Khushboo Maken Sood")
```

Here, the `must` operator will take the result returned by the `getFullName` method and pass it to the Matcher, which in this case is `beEqualTo`.

Let's look at different types of Matchers in more detail.

Simple Matchers

We saw an example of this in our last example, that is `beEqualTo`. This is also the most common type of Matcher.

Here are a few of the syntaxes of equality Matchers:

Matcher	Comment
`'x' must beEqualTo('x')`	Normal equals Matcher
`'x' must be_==('x')`	With a symbol
`'x' must_== 'x'`	Quite popular and succinct
`'x' mustEqual 'x'`	Without underscore
`'x' should_== 'x'`	If you like should

`'x' === 'x'`	The shortcut way
`'x' must be equalTo('x')`	More verbose and readable

There are some additional concepts of equality:

Matcher	Comment
`beTypedEqualTo`	Typed equality operator. This will not work if a and b are of discordant types
`be_===`	Similar to `beTypedEqualTo`
`a === b`	Same as a must `beTypedQualTo(b)`
`a must_=== b`	This is the same as `must_==` b. The only difference being that there is no type check if a and b are of different types
`be_==~`	Much fancier. It checks that provided there is an implicit conversion conv from a to b, then `(a: A) == conv(b: B)`
`beTheSameAs`	Reference equality
`be`	Same as `beTheSameAs`
`beTrue, beFalse`	Used for Boolean equality

Be aware that `beEqualTo` Matcher is akin to the normal `==` Scala equality operator and has the same behavior and limitations.

There are some other Matchers that fall under the category of inequality Matchers:

Matcher	Usage example
`must not be equalTo`	`name must not be equalTo("Joe")`
`must !=`	`name must != "Joe"`
`mustNotEqual`	`name mustNotEqual "Joe"`
`must be !=`	`name must be != ("Joe")`
`!==`	`name !== "Joe"`

Matchers for strings

Specs2 has a plethora of Matchers that are there specially for matching strings or are a part of a string. This includes checking for substrings or comparing the string against powerful (or trivial) regular expressions:

Matcher	Usage example
.ignoreCase	"Sweden" must beEqualTo("Sweden").ignoreCase
.ignoreSpace	"Japan" must beEqualTo(" Japan").ignoreSpace
.ignoreCase.ignoreSpace	"Japan" must beEqualTo(" Japan ").ignoreSpace.ignoreCase
contains	"Russia" must contain ("sia")
startsWith	"Shimla" must startWith ("Shi")
endsWith	"England" must endWith ("and")
not startsWith	"England" must not startWith("Eng")
have size	"Shimla" must have size(6)
beMatching	"Shimla" must beMatching ("S\\w{4}a") "Shimla" must beMatching ("""S\w{4}a""")
=~	"Japan" must =~("""J\w{3}n""")
find and withGroups	"Korea" must find("""(or.)""").withGroups("rea")

Many of these Matchers are palpable. We can also use the `must beMatching(...)` method. In the preceding examples, we are using both regular and raw strings eliminating the need for escaping the backslash. `beMatching` is similar to the `=~`. `Spec2`. The string Matchers can also match a substring or a regular expression group.

Matchers for relational operators

Relational operators in Scala can either have a more DSL-like syntax or can just be symbolic objects:

Matcher	Usage example
be_<	ageOfApplicant should be_<(50)
not be_>	ageOfApplicant should not be_>(50)

beLessThan	ageOfApplicant must beLessThan(50)
be_>	ageOfApplicant should be_>(3)
beGreaterThan	ageOfApplicant must beGreaterThan(3)
be_<=	ageOfApplicant should be_<=(100)
beLessThanOrEqualTo	ageOfApplicant must beLessThanOrEqualTo(100)
be_>=	ageOfApplicant should be_>=(0)
beGreaterThanOrQualTo	ageOfApplicant must beGreaterThanOrEqualTo(0)
===	ageOfApplicant === (42)

Matchers for floating point

Specs2 offers proximity Matchers for floating point calculations to cater for loss of precision:

Matchers	Usage examples
be_==	(1.2 + 1.3) must be_==(2.5)
beCloseTo	(1.2 + 1.3) must beCloseTo (2.5, 0.01)
not beCloseTo	(1.2 + 1.3) must not beCloseTo (3.5, 0.01)
not be closeTo	(1.2 + 1.3) must not be closeTo (3.5, 0.01)

Matchers for references

Matcher	Usage example
beTheSameAs	circle must beTheSameAs(shape)
Not beTheSameAs	orange must not beTheSameAs(shape)

Matchers for Option/Either

There are a few Matchers, which are specifically used for `Option` and `Either`:

Matcher	Usage example
beSome	`result must beSome("Result")`
beNone	`result must not beNone`
beRight	`result must beRight`

Matchers for the try monad

There are few Matchers that are specific for use with `try`:

Matcher	Comment
beSuccessfulTry	This checks if the result is `Success(_)`. It can be combined with `withValue` to check for the actual value.
beFailedTry	This will check if the result is `Failure(_)`. It can be combined with a `withThrowable` to verify the exception.

Matching exception

Specs2 has a very succinct way of checking that an exception is thrown:

- `throwA[ExceptionType]`
- `throwAExceptionType`
- `throwA(exception)`

Iterable Matchers

These Matchers are mostly the same as the ones used in ScalaTest for matching iterables, except for some interesting new versions:

Matcher	Usage example
empty	`(Nil must be).empty`
Not be empty	`List(4, 5, 6) should not be empty`

not contains	List(4, 5, 6) must not contain(3)
contain	List (4, 5, 6) must contain(4)
only.inOrder	List(1,8,9) should contain (1,8,9).only.inOrder
inOrder	List(0, 1, 2, 3, 4, 5, 6) must contain (3, 4, 5).inOrder
have size	List(5, 6) must have size(2)
Lave length	List(9, 8, 7) must have length (3)

Matchers for sequences and traversables

Specs2 contains some unique Matchers for verifying conditions for seq and traversables:

Matcher	Usage example
onlyOnce	List("Welcome", "Home") should containMatch("Wel").onlyOnce
containPattern	List("Welcome", "Home") should containPattern(".*ome") List("Welcome", "Home") should containPattern("\\w{4}")
containMatch	List("Welcome", "Home") should containMatch("lc") List("Welcome", "Home") should containMatch("Welcome")
haveTheSameElementsAs	List("Welcome", "Home") should haveTheSameElementsAs(List("Welcome", "Home"))
have	List("Welcome", "Home") should have(_.size >= 4)

containMatch is used to determine if any of the elements of the sequence contain the string. containPattern is used to match the elements of the sequence against a regular expression. onlyOnce is used for asserting that the contains match only occurs once in the sequence. The have Matcher accepts a Boolean function, which is asserted over all the elements of the sequence. All the elements of the sequence must adhere to the Boolean function in the have Matcher. The haveTheSameElementsAs Matcher matches the sequence on the left with the sequence on the right.

Matchers for maps

These Matchers are quite straightforward. You can find out if the map has a specific key, value, or a pair of key/value. You can also check for absence of these:

Matcher	Usage example
haveKey	employeeMap must haveKey("Name")
haveValue	employeeMap must haveValue("Joe")
Not haveKey	employeeMap must not haveKey("Roll Number")
Not haveValue	employeeMap must not haveKey("James Bond")
havePair	employeeMap must havePair("Name" -> "Joe Bloggs")

Matchers for XML

Specs2 comes bundled with syntactic sugar for matching XML elements. This can disregard any whitespaces. Scala also has a built-in support for XML. Scala is able to parse a XML representing each XML element as an `Elem` object.

First thought, which may come to your mind, is why don't we use string Matchers to match XMLs. Well you can do it if the literal string representations of the two XMLs is same, including all the whitespaces and so on. Secondly, the message you would get back if the XMLs are not equal is also not a very useful one.

To use the XML Matchers to match whole XMLS, simply use `beEqualToIgnoringSpace` instead of `beEqualTo` and `be_==\` instead of `be_==`.

Alternatively, you can use normal Matchers to match the `Elem` object, which is returned by Scala's built-in XML capabilities.

Matchers for files

Specs2 more or less mimics the Java API for files to provide Matchers.

Matcher	Comments
beEqualToIgnoringSep	This checks if two paths are the same, regardless of the drive separator `d:`
beAReadablePath	This verifies if the path is readable

beAnAbsolutePath	This verifies if the path is an absolute path
beAnExistingPath	This checks if the given path exists
beAWriteablePath	This verifies whether the path is writeable
beAHiddenPath	This verifies whether the path is hidden
beADirectoryPath	This verifies the path is a directory
beAFilePath	This verifies if the path is a file
haveAnAbsolutePath	This verifies if the path has an absolute path
havePathName	This verifies whether the path has a name or not
haveAParentPath	This verifies if the path has a parent path
haveName	This verifies that the file has the given name
listPaths	This verifies if the given has the given list of children
beHidden	This verifies if the file is hidden
beWriteable	This verifies if the file is writeable
exists	This verifies whether the file exists

Matchers for partial functions

Partial functions are very important features of any functional language. In Scala, they are used to control whether a predicate pertains to its input and, if it does, then run the code inside the function. There are two Matchers that are used for matching partial functions; beDefinedAt and beDefinedBy. Let's look at an example to better understand this:

```scala
val kidPartialFunction: PartialFunction[String, Int] = new
PartialFunction[String, Int] {

  def apply(v1: Int) = "Kid"

  def isDefinedAt(x: Int) = x <= 16
}

val seniorPartialFunction: PartialFunction[String, Int] =
{case x: Int if
    (x >= 60) => "Senior"}
val adultPartialFunction: PartialFunction[String, Int] =
{case x: Int if
    (x >=16 && x < 60) => "Adult"}
```

```
val classification = kidPartialFunction
    orElse seniorPartialFunction orElse adultPartialFunction
classification must beDefinedAt (10)
classification must beDefinedBy (65 -> "Senior")
classification must beDefinedBy (23 -> "Adult")
```

You can very well appreciate the usefulness of a partial function from the given example. Here we want to classify people into kids, adults, and seniors, depending on their age. We can chain them all into a single call classification.

The preceding example explains the use of Matchers `beDefinedAt` and `beDefinedBy` to verify the partial functions.

Other Matchers

Specs2 is extremely flexible about Matchers and allows creation of custom Matchers if required. Let's look at creating our own Matcher, which will check if the number is an odd number:

```
def beOdd: Matcher[Int] = (i: Int) => (i % 2 == 1, i+" is odd", i+" is
even")
```

Specs2 data tables

Data tables in Specs2 are similar to the table in table-driven property checks. The table consists of a sample input value and an expected result. A function test case follows the table that is run for each row of the table with inputs acting as input to the function, and the result of the function is verified with the expected output in the table:

```
package com.packt

import org.specs2.matcher.DataTables
import org.specs2.Specification

class EmployeeAgeSpecification extends Specification
with DataTables {def is =
  "Trying out a table of values for testing purposes to
  determine the age of an  employee".name ^
  """The first column is the employee first name,
  the second is a employee last name,
    and third is Year of Birth
    and the forth column is the
```

```
        expected age in 2016""" ! employeeTable

    def employeeTable =
        "First Name" | "Last Name"         | "Year Of Birth" |   "Age"|
        "Joe"          !! "Blogs"            !1980 !              36    |
        "Khushboo"     !! "Sood"        !1984    !       32|
        "Johan"        !! "Sood"          ! 2013    !      3|
        "Jairus"       !! "Sood"           !2016     !     0| > {
        (x:String, y:String, z:Int, p:Int) ⇒
        new Employee(x, y, z).ageTill(2016) must_== p
    }
}
```

In the preceding example, it can be seen that the input values from column 1, 2, and 3 of the data table are fed as input to the test, and the result is compared against the value in column 4.

Running Specs2 tests

SBT recognizes Specs2 as a **test framework**; therefore, it is the most common way to run Specs2 tests. The fact that SBT considers Specs2 a test framework enables SBT to execute any class or object that is extending the `Specification` abstract class. The test target of SBT will execute any specification within the `src/test/scala` directory:

sbt> test

You can also run individual tests using the `test-only` target:

sbt> test-only org.packt. EmployeeAgeDataTableSpecification

Summary

Specs2 is an equally popular and powerful test framework as ScalaTest for unit testing Scala application code. There are both pros and cons of using Specs2. There are some benefits like and extensive choice of Matchers and running parallel tests. More than the actual benefits, it boils down to individual preference whether to use Specs2 or ScalaTest.

9
Miscellaneous and Emerging Trends in Scala TDD

We just skimmed the surface of the testing technologies and processes in the previous chapters. If you are or have been a developer for some time now, you would agree that no one technology or process is best. There are always refinements and something better coming up. Let's briefly touch on some of the bits that may be useful in future. In this chapter, we will be covering the following:

- Scala Futures and Promises
- Inside trait
- Option values
- Either values
- Eventually and integration patience
- Consumer-Driven Contracts

Scala Futures and Promises

Futures in Scala are an extension of Futures in Java. They allow us to execute multiple tasks in parallel in a very efficient and non-blocking manner. Just like in Java, the Future is a placeholder of a result of a computation that has been run asynchronously. Normally, the result of the asynchronous computation is supplied to the Future in a concurrent manner. This results in a non-blocking asynchronous task. Scala Futures provide methods that can be used to check when the concurrent task is finished.

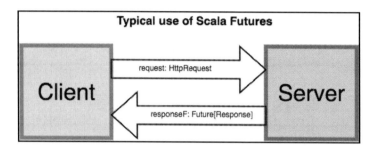

The default behavior of Futures and Promises is that they are non-blocking operations and provide callbacks for getting the results of the asynchronous task. In Scala, we can make use of methods such as `flatMap`, `filter`, and `foreach` to use the Futures in a non-blocking manner.

Let's look at some examples here:

```
Val studentFuture:Future[StudentDetails] {
    // non-blocking rest call or computation
    studentService.studentDetails('Student 101')
} (executionContext)
```

Another way of writing this example would be:

```
Implicit val ec:ExecutionContext = ...
Val studentFuture:Future[StudentDetails] {
    // non-blocking rest call or computation
    studentService.studentDetails('Student 101')
} //ec is passed implicitly
```

In both of these examples, the running of the non-blocking computation is delegated to `ExecutionContext` and the result of the Future is inside `studentFuture`.

ExecutionContext

`ExecutionContext` is responsible for executing the non-blocking (usually) task. If you have used Executors in Java then you can draw a parallel between `ExecutionContext` and Executors. `ExecutionContext`-like Executor is responsible for running the task in a separate thread.

Scala also provides a global execution context, `ExecutionContext.global`. `ExecutionContext` is supported by `ForkJoinPool`, which is an implementation of the `ExecutorService` interface from Java. The `ForkJoinPool` framework exists so you can take the benefit of multiple processors.

`ForkJoinPool` manages the restricted number of threads, this number is also known as parallelism level and is dependent on the number of processors. `ExecutionContext.global` sets the parallelism level to default to the number of processors unless otherwise specified.

Futures

`Future` in Scala (and also in Java) is an object that holds a value, which is not yet available and is computed in a separate non-blocking task that is being run by `ExecutionContext`. `Future` is referred to as "completed" when the task has finished and the result is available in the `Future`. Otherwise, if the task is not yet finished, then the `Future` is "not completed."

The value which the `Future` holds can only be assigned to it once. When the `Future` object gets a value or alternatively an exception, it becomes immutable:

```
import scala.concurrent._
import ExecutionContext.Implicits.global

val session = EmployeeService.session
val employeeFuture: Future[List[Employee]] = Future {
  session.getAllEmployees()
}
```

We need to import `scala.concurrent._` package to get access to `Future`. As explained in the previous section, `ExecutionContext.Implicits.global` imports the default global `ExecutionContext`.

Callbacks on the `Future` objects are used to define the task that would be run on when the value is available in the `Future` (it is completed). The most general way of defining a callback is to use `onComplete`. This creates a callback function of type `Try[T] => U`. If `Future` completes successfully, then this callback is applied to a value of type `Success[T]`. Alternatively, if there is an exception during execution of the non-blocking task, then a value of type `Failure[T]` is applied:

```scala
import scala.util.{Success, Failure}
import scala.concurrent._
import ExecutionContext.Implicits.global

val session = EmployeeService.session
val employeeFuture: Future[List[Employee]] = Future {
  session.getAllEmployees()
}

employeeFuture onComplete {
  case Success(employees) => for (employee <- employees)
    println(employee.getFullName)
  case Failure(t) => println("An error has occured: " + t.getMessage)
}
```

Instead of using `onComplete,` we can also use `onSuccess` and/or `onFailure` callbacks:

```scala
employeeFuture onFailure {
  case t => println("An error has occured: " + t.getMessage)
}
employeeFuture onSuccess {
  case Success(employees) => for (employee <- employees)
    println(employee.getFullName)
}
```

More in-depth details about Scala Futures and Promises are available at ht tp://danielwestheide.com/blog/2013/01/16/the-neophytes-guide-t o-scala-part-9-promises-and-futures-in-practice.html.

The Inside trait

ScalaTest contains an `Inside` trait. This feature, in turn, includes an `inside` construct. This construct is used to make assertions about the object graphs, which are nested. You can use pattern matching to do this.

Let's look at an example. Suppose, we have these case classes:

```
case class College(name:String, city:String, ranking:String)
case class Student(fName:String, lName:String, rollNo:String)
case class CollegeRecord(student:Student, college:College)
```

Then, we can write specifications like this:

```
inside (cRec) { case CollegeRecord(student, college) =>
   inside (student) { case Student(fName, lName, rollNo) =>
        fName should be ("Johan")
        lName should be ("Sood")
        rollNo should be ("CTEC03812")
   }
   inside(college) { case College(name, city, ranking) =>
        name should be ("California Tech")
        city should be("Sacramento")
        ranking should be ("1")
   }
}
```

In the case of a failure of an assertion, the `Inside` trait provides descriptive messages, which are formed using the `toString` implementation of the objects, passed to the `inside` clause. Let us look at an example of this.

If the object under test is:

```
val cRec = CollegeRecord(
   Student("Jairus", "Sood", "CTEC03812"),
   College("California Tech", "Sacramento", "1")
)
```

Then, we will get this error message:

"J[airus]" was not equal to "Johan[]", inside Student(Jairus, Sood, CTEC03812),
inside CollegeRecord(Student(Jairus, Sood, CTEC03812), College("California Tech", "Sacramento",
"1"))

The OptionValue trait

By including the OptionValue trait in our mixin, we get an implicit conversion of Option. This implicit conversion adds a value method to Option. The value method either returns the value from a defined option or alternatively throws TestFailedException in case the Option is not defined.

Using this, we are able to test in a single expression both that the Option is defined and also that it has a certain expected value. Let's look at an example:

```
val opt:Option[String] = Some("Star Trek")
```

Our test is as follows:

```
opt.value.length should be > 5
```

Alternatively, we can have an assertion here like:

```
assert(opt.value.length > 5)
```

If we were using a standard get method on the option to get the value, we would get a NoSuchElementException. Therefore by using the OptionValue trait we are able to reduce the verbosity of our test and eliminate some boilerplate code; for example:

```
val anotherOpt: Option[String] = None

anotherOpt.get .length should be > 5
```

Here, anotherOpt.get will throw NoSuchElementException. This will make the test fail, but it wouldn't specify appropriately which line in the test caused the failure. *Au contraire*, the stack trace we get from TestFailedException, when we use the OptionValue trait, has precise information about which line in the test code is responsible for the test failure.

We can also receive the same result (though a lot more verbose), using two tests instead of one, for example:

```
val yetAnotherOpt: Option[String] = None

yetAnotherOpt should be ('defined)
yetAnotherOpt.get.length should be > 5
```

Here, we had to split our test in two to get the same result we could get from the OptionValue trait in one single expression.

The EitherValue trait

By including the `EitherValue` trait in our mixin, we get an implicit conversion of the `Either` monad. This implicit conversion adds a value method to both left and right of `Either`. This allows us to do a `left.value` and `right.value`. The `value` method either returns the selected value from a defined `Either` or alternatively throws a `TestFailedException` in case the `Either` is not defined.

Using this, we are able to test in a single expression, both that the `Either` should be left or right (that is, it is defined) and also that it has a certain expected value. Let's look at an example:

```
firstEither.right.value should be < 5
secondEither.left.value should be ("Big Ploblemo!")
```

The same can be done using assertions:

```
assert(firstEither.right.value should be < 5)
assert(secondEither.left.value === "Big Ploblemo!")
```

If we were using a standard `right.get` and `left.get` method on the `Either` to get the value, we would get a `NoSuchElementException`. Therefore, using the `EitherValue` trait, we are able to reduce the verbosity of our test and eliminate some boilerplate code, for example:

```
val thirdEither: Either[Int, Float] = Left("Big Problemo!")
thirdEither.right.get should be < 5
```

This will throw `NoSuchElementException`. It will make the test fail but it wouldn't specify appropriately which line in the test caused the failure. *Au contraire*, the stack trace we get from `TestFailedException`, when we use the `EitherValue` trait, has detailed information about which line in the test code is responsible for the test failure.

We can also receive the same result (though a lot more verbose) using two tests instead of one, for example:

```
val yetAnotherEither: Either[Int, String] = Left("You have a Problem!!")

yetAnotherEither should be ('right)
yetAnotherEither.right.get.length should be < 5
```

Here, we had to split our test in two to get the same result we could get from the `OptionValue` trait in one single expression.

Eventually

The Eventually trait provides an `eventually` method, which can repeatedly execute a function passed by name. This is done until the passed function succeeds or the timeout, which was configured, has been exceeded.

The function, which was passed by name, is considered to "succeed" when it returns a result. If the function throws an exception, then eventually will "fail" and would result in the failure of the test.

Let's look at a few examples of `eventually`. Let's see a successful example first:

```
val alphabets = 'a' to 'z'
val iterator = alphabets.iterator
eventually { iterator.next should be ('p') }
```

The default timeout for eventually is 150 milliseconds. This means that if we use the following code, it would result in `TestFailedDueToTimeoutException`:

```
val alphabets = 'a' to 'z'
val iterator = alphabets.iterator
eventually { Thread.sleep(50); iterator.next should be ('p') }
```

How to configure eventually

The configuration of the `eventually` method is quite flexible. There are two parameters that can be used to configure eventually. These are as follows:

- `timeout`: The default value is `scaled(150 milliseconds)`. It is used to set the maximum time up to which the named function can result in unsuccessful attempts.
- `interval`: The default value is `scaled(15 milliseconds)`. This is the sleep interval between each iteration/attempt.

There is an implicit method which is passed to all the `eventually` methods of the `Eventually` trait. This parameter is a `PatienceConfig` object. There are two parameters, which are used to configure the `PatienceConfig`. These parameters are also called "patience" because they determine how tolerant the test will be.

There is an implicit `val patienceConfig` in the trait `Eventually`. The configuration parameters of this `patienceConfig` is set to the default value (150 `milliseconds` and 15 `milliseconds`). To customize the value of any of these parameters, we can override the `patienceConfig` implicit `val`.

Let's see as an example if we want to set the default timeout of 5 seconds and the default interval of 3 milliseconds:

```
implicit override val patienceConfig =
  PatienceConfig(timeout = scaled(Span(5, Seconds)), interval =
scaled(Span(3,
  Millis)))
```

There are some overloaded implementations of `eventually`, which allow us to change both or one of the timeout and interval for a single invocation of eventually, for example:

Change timeout:

```
eventually (timeout(Span(2, Seconds))) { iterator.next should be ('p') }
```

Change interval:

```
eventually (interval(Span(3, Millis))) { iterator.next should be ('p') }
```

or change both:

```
eventually (timeout(Span(2, Seconds)), interval(Span(3, Millis)))
{ iterator.next should be ('p') }
```

Simple backoff algorithm

There is a very simple backoff algorithm, which is used by the `eventually` method to increase the speed of the test. Since the operation run inside eventually is asynchronous, if it completes quickly, then the interval can be smaller. On the contrary, if the operation takes more time, then if the interval is small, it will utilize precious CPU time by continuously checking and rechecking for a result that is not available.

A middle ground between these two tradeoffs is reached where the checks done by the `eventually` method are more frequent during the initial interval. During the initial interval, instead of sleeping for the entire duration of the interval, `eventually` will sleep for only 1/10th of the duration. This is done for the first interval, after that `eventually` sleeps for the configured interval.

Integration patience

Even though `eventually` allows for the default timeout to be configured for a unit test the use of `Eventually` for unit testing should be questioned. Unit tests should always be designed and written with speed in mind. They are designed to be a way of giving an instantaneous result, so it can be fixed easily. When unit testing, we would normally use mock objects to remove dependencies from subsystems. Saying this, you would eventually end up using `Eventually` for a unit test in cases where it fits better. Therefore, the default values of patience are configured for use with unit tests.

If we are using `Eventually` for integration testing, the default timeout and interval are too small. The best way to override these is by mixing in the `IntegrationPatience` trait, for example:

```
class PacktSpec extends FeatureSpec with Eventually with
IntegrationPatience {
  // Out integration tests goes here...
}
```

The `IntegrationPatience` trait is configured to increase the default timeout from `150 milliseconds` to `15 seconds`. It is also configured to increase the default value of interval from `15 milliseconds` to `150 milliseconds`. If it is required, we can still customize the value of these two patience configurations.

Consumer-Driven Contracts

There are quite a few patterns, which dictate the communication between dissimilar modules. This becomes especially useful in microservice architecture.

 You can learn more about microservices at `http://martinfowler.com/articles/microservices.html`.

Consumer-Driven Contracts (CDC) is a one of these patterns. It specifies how different modules of the application will interact. The fact that this pattern is called consumer-driven, means that it is the liability of the consumer of the service to dictate what kind of interaction it is expecting and the format this interaction should be in. All the other services (providers) must agree to these contracts and make sure that they are abiding by them.

These contracts from the consumer enable us to understand the business importance and value from the perspective of the consumer. The consumer's contracts, through the assertions and expectations, define which bits of the provider's contract of service support the business value expected by the system.

The trite explanation of consumer-driven provider agreements augments an autocratic facet to the association between service provider and consumer. This means that the provider is obligated to the requirements that actually arise from outside of its confines. It's worth noting, that this does not voilate the primarily sovereign nature of the provider or the principles of separation of concerns. It merely makes bare the point that the success of the service depends on the consumers of the service.

Characteristics of CDC:

- **Self-contained and thorough**:

  A consumer-driven contract should be self-contained and thorough. This means that it should cover all the functionality, which is demanded by the existing consumers. The contract also signifies the full and compulsory set of exportable rudiments that are needed to provision the expectations of the clients.

- **Extraordinary and non-authoritative**:

  The contracts of the providers are unparalleled in their countenance of the business values available to the system, but non-fixative because these values are consequent from the amalgamation of existing consumer anticipations.

- **Constrained constancy and immutability**:

  A consumer-driven contract is supposed to be unchanging and firm. This means that we can ascertain the validity of the consumer-driven contract as per the given set of consumer contracts. The contracts are subject to modification as expectations are mutated.

How services interface with each other

The following two ways explain how to interface services with each other.

The gigantic way

In a typical monolithic application, all the modules live together alongside each other. What separates them is the fact that they may be in different packages or JARs.

In this particular case, the Integration tests between services/ modules can be done practically like regular unit tests. Here, the modules which are under test get their dependent modules instantiated and injected at runtime. These tests not only assert the fact that the modules are interacting with each other as expected or dictated by the API but also that the functional requirements are met. The compiler also helps as it will reject the tests if the method signature or the API has changed and the change was not propagated throughout the system.

Microservices

In this case, different services are not wired together or co-exist in the same JVM. These services can be deployed separately in geographically diverse locations. Here, the changes in the provider service are not caught by the compiler of the consumer service, for example:

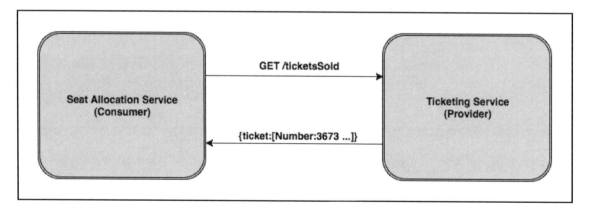

In this example, the **Ticketing Service** and the **Seat Allocation Service** are both separate services in different JVM. The consumer (**Seating Allocation Service**) makes a rest call to the provider (**Ticketing Service**) to determine the number and type of tickets that have been sold.

Without any form of format service contract between the two, the service agreement can be easily broken if the **Ticketing Service** changes the API or the schema of the result. Some of the common ways that the provider can change its interface are:

- Changing the parameters required to make the rest call, for example, **/ticketsSold** requires a new mandatory field "date"
- Changing the rest endpoint, for example, **/ticketsSold** is renamed to **/ticketsSoldInformation**
- Change in the schema of the response payload, for example, instead of JSON, the provider changes to return XML

Even thought the preceding changes look like major breaking changes and should make more noise, there can be some subtle changes in the application code of the provider that can result in change in the schema of the output. It can be something as simple as changing a field name in a class from in which JSON is constructed.

If it was a monolithic system, then the compiler would have caught this change immediately; but in this case, there is no such safeguard. Both the consumer and the provider service will run smoothly without any runtime errors until the time the actual rest call is made. This may lead to some time-consuming debugs from the consumer service before realizing that the error is actually because of extraneous changes.

Using CDC to integrate microservices

Traditional way

The most obvious way to test the compatibility between two services is to start them both and verify that the communication between them is happening as expected. There are some issues which these approach, primarily that one service does not have control over the start and stop of another service. So both services may not be available at the same time for verification. This verification also seems more reactive rather than proactive. The consumer service will notice the changes from the provider and then make retrospective changes to its API, so it conforms to the changes from the provider.

Using CDC

In the traditional perspective explained in the previous section, the provider is free to make changes independent of realizing whether or not these changes are affecting or relevant to the consumer. This seems to break the notion that the provider is providing a service for the consumer.

The idea behind CDC is to split the work of integration testing right in the middle where the communication between the two services takes place:

1. The consumer of the service will dictate what it requires from a particular request to the provider.
2. Both the provider and the consumer would agree to this contract of service.
3. The provider has integration tests at its end to verify that it is satisfying the contract at all times.
4. This entails a few changes from the traditional approach:
   - There needs to be a ubiquitous language or a way for the consumer to define what it needs from the provider. Therefore, the consumer will need a way to publish contracts.
   - Providers will need to be able to know where these contracts are published and how to read and verify them.
   - Both the parties need to decide on some form of mutual state.

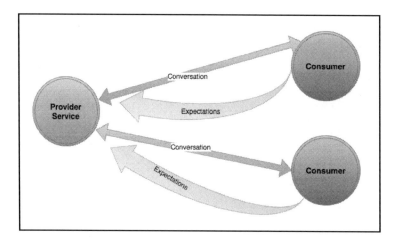

Benefits of CDC

- Services are not dependent on each other for their implementation. One service does not require the other to be running for it to be able to perform integration testing. In fact, both the services can be developed together as the contract eliminates the need for coexistence of the services. It can be the case that the provider has not been developed while the consumer is being written. As long as the provider confirms to the contract, the services are bound to work together.
- The consumer of the service is responsible for establishment and continuation of the contract. This shifts the onus of the viability of the service from the provider to the consumer. Since the consumers create the contracts, the provider ends up creating a service that provides better business value.
- Provider's application code is more resilient to changes. This means that since the service provided by the provider is bounded by the contracts which are maintained by the consumer, when the provider make changes to its application code, all it needs to do is to verify that it is still conforming to the contract to ascertain that everything is acceptable.

Summary

We looked at some aspects of unit testing with Scala in this book. My recommendation to the readers is to watch this space. There are new processes and technologies coming up almost every day in this space. Scala, in my opinion, is the new Java and the hype won't die. It will continue to encompass more and more aspects of development. The fact that Scala now has a open source community which is larger than what Java once had should give you a gist of how big it will be.

I have also seen unit testing come from a place of infancy to now being a mature principle with more and more people adopting it as a standard. It is no coincidence that Scala comes with such a mature arsenal of unit testing technologies. It had the added benefit of being able to stand on the shoulders of the giant. This giant is the unit testing frameworks already in the market for Java and other languages.

Index

32511614R00109

Printed in Great Britain
by Amazon

CONTENTS

A HARVEST OF WHEAT

All day the sounds of scythes
Cutting stalks. Our hands sticky
With juices, our arms heavy
With swathes of wheat.

All day in the blazing sun.
Our backs arched, eyes focused
On the sharp blade and the stems.
Slicing and gathering systematically.

All day in a kind of communion:
My father reciting the Koran;
My brothers and cousins and nephews
Exchanging stories and jokes. Our lives

Inter-mingling, growing around words.
Above us, the crows caw all day.
By evening there are bales of wheat
Scattered in an open field.

The women near the edges make
Nan bread. The scent of dough,
Baking, comforts our exhausted bodies.
Embers float up into the navy sky.

One by one stars begin to glimmer.
We navigate ourselves towards Mecca.
My father's voice rises between us.
His words crumble in my mouth.

The Chucky

My grandmother straddles
Around the chucky. She funnels
A handful of maize into the hole

Then she turns the upper slab
Clockwise, just as her mother used to.
Sometimes she feels the grainy texture

Of her grandmother's palm, sometimes
The flexible and awkward energy
Of young eager hands. Once

Light spilt from between the slabs
Of the chucky and the mud dried room
Filled with the spirits of all our mothers.

Voices spoke, voices hummed, voices
Sang of lush gardens, wondrous
And rich, of undying streams

And fountains that poured clear honey.
But usually all she can see
Is her aging hand, all she can feel

Is an aching absence. My mother
Has a Philips grinder and my sister
Knows how to change the fuse.

And when they make maize rotti
We always have it with spinach
And lots of butter. Sometimes the scents

Swivel my grandmother's elbow
Before our eyes and we recall
The story of how our mother

Ran in with dad to tell
Her mum of their plans to go to England
How the grinding stopped and the flour

Spilt and the sudden silence
Was interrupted by a gust
Which shut the door on the light.

WHEAT IN MAY

Wind swirls around her
Surges among the mass of wheat
Becomes an emerald
Tidal wave as millions of heads
Nod and sway.
Shrieking parrots thump
From the rippling stalks
Into the blue May. She laughs,
As if drunk, feeling the wheat
Brush her bosoms and tiny feet
Kick her from inside.

SARDAR, LAHORE

I

Today the colour of sunlight
Is of warm halva
And of my skin
And of that steamy pile
From which worms writhe.

My cousin hides
Behind his mother's arms.
Nothing of this will be said
To anyone. The untouchables
Will be paid accordingly.

II

I turn the handle of the Singer machine
And watch the needle go clean
Through nail and hit bone. Slowly
I move the wheel back.
My left forefinger lifts
With the needle. Gently
I ease it free. Blood oozes
From that black hole.
My brother has run away from home.
I will look for him, once
I have cleaned the machine.

III

I am honeycombed
By the hard shadow of the tracery window.
I sit on the stone floor and eat ripe plums.

Slowly the shadow begins to slant
Slowly it tapers and becomes
A frayed rope of light.

In the corner granma is crumpled up in bed.
Her stick-like figure makes dunes of the sheets.
Slowly her face disappears.

SADAREH

My grandmother lightly touches her eyes.
A thin opaque film has formed on both.
Her stringy arms shake a little.

A tree full of birds, such as this one,
Has the presence of many souls.

Bothered by the chatter of the birds
I take a large stick and the constant
Chiming, spirits singing,
Brass bells ringing stops.

BAJDA RIDGE

All the lemons in the tree
Gleam like lots of little suns
And the leaves purse kisses to the wind.
A blue bag flaps under a rock
As a man works a rotovator
Across a field; in close step behind him
A woman scatters seed.
Behind them there is a hut
Whose roof is lined with fat pumpkins.
In the field beyond two boys and a girl
Drag cabbages. I snuff up aniseed
And diesel, just then
From a furrow by my foot, a brown bird
Scutters off; one feather glints
Like the tip of a plough.

ON THE 43 TO THE TERMINUS

It's Manchester weather in Malta.
The rickety bus, packed with tourists,
Thunders towards Valletta.
Just above the driver is written,
"Think God," and the way he took
That last corner we all did.

Our combined breathing
Has steamed up the windows.
I keep nodding off and each time
I surface, for some reason, I know
The exact nature of the conversation
The Germans, behind me, are having.
I stop myself short from speaking
To them in my Mancunian English.

The little Maltese girl, in the lap
Of her mum sat in front of me,
Has drawn lots of tiny hearts
On the window. Briefly I press
My palm over the hearts just
As the bus bulldozes into Valletta station.
The fine contours of my print
Map out five tiny islands
And a fat V-shaped peninsula.
Something of me in an ocean of mist.

The windows clear as we disembark.

My Hands

All day I have wiped paste inks
From auxiliary rollers, ink ducts,
Rubber stamps and the work top; dabbing
My fingers in trichloroethane.

The cleaning solution is clear as water
And smells like methylated spirits.
My fingers are numb. When I squeeze them
They tingle, letting loose

Tiny electric bolts. The top part
Of the fingerprints are grained with inks.
My fingers are like lighthouses
Granulating under a storm of acids.

Fissures straddle across them.
Some cuts run deep as valleys. The air
In them is loaded with missile-shaped atoms
That bombard the surface.

Dust plumes up. I shed flesh flakes.
My hands are ageing, faster
Than the rest of me; look
They are like two finished pages of a diary.

Mr Khan

Cleans his good printing machine
Utters a little prayer
And starts the first job slow.
I am warming her up before we really go.

As the counter ticks
And the rollers turn
Mr Khan expresses disgust, about some Asians
He has seen, in Whalley Range,
Driving Mercedes and squandering money on lust.

Mr Khan mounts the machine
And runs her fast, watches
The rollers print, the waste paper peel, listens
To the counter ticking
And observes the first reel
Finished at last.

It is time for mid-day prayer.
Mr Khan washes his feet, face, hands and elbows.
He must be clean before God.

He turns his face to Mecca
And bows to Allah
And between Mr Khan and Mecca
Is the huge printing machine
Humming to itself hymns
Counting sticky labels for knickers
For the bottoms of healthy girls.

Mr Khan's paper face creases
And sweats;
He inks the air red
With the print of his prayers
His prayers for, his daughter,
His daughter's bones that are
Ungluing marrow…

Mr Khan peels away from God
And tends to the machine

This is a very nice machine, pays me good money
I will be shopping at Tesco's tonight.

FOR M

I smell of paste inks and cleaning
Solutions. The ghost vapours of
The printing machine I have hurriedly
Cleaned. I'm rushing

Through traffic to get home
To you. This is the third
Traffic light I have jumped.
Now I am, running through

Your hall, entering the lounge –
Sunshine – and you a static
Silhouette by the window. Your
Hand is cool dew in my

Flushing palm. You are
Morning fresh jasmines. I am
Acid on metal. We mix
In the steam of stew, the vapour of wine.

"Can you see there is too much water here
I'm looking at you mum, from another shore."
"How did this happen?" she asks in fear.

"I really don't know, it's just not clear
But we're living in London not Lahore.
Can you see there is too much water here

Between us;" my father's voice thunders near
My trembling heart. "Leper – you're unpure."
"How did this happen?" she asks in fear.

"Blood is thicker than water – do you hear.
United in marriage." "I'm not so sure
Can you see there is too much water here

It's unbridgable. We'll be divorced in a year."
"Rubbish you are filth – corrupt to the core."
"How did this happen?" she asks in fear.

Behind my sore eyes wells a large bitter tear
If I go, just go, then home is no more.
"Can you see there is too much water here."
"How did this happen?" she asks in fear.

A Curry of Lamb and Turnips

The lamb chunks are like chopped wood
Among a cover of leafy brown turnips.
The melting butter is a flow of sunshine.
I savour each mouthful, chewing slowly
All the colours of autumn:
Mellowed out saffron, ground red peppers,
Grainy sinews of meat and ginger,
Soft tissues of garlic and turnips.

Turnips hand pulled by women in grubby sarees
From a field which is close to a forest.
Among the trees, silence, autumn heat
And the dark silhouette of the woman
Of my dreams. When she moves
She creates cool currents of air. I think
To touch her and the forest winters out
And I find myself alone in my mother's kitchen
With a cold unfinished curry.

THE MINISTER'S GARDEN
On a painting by Cecile Lawson

I

The three fat hives have porous pots for hats
And straw as a careless fringe. Their minds
Have formulated ambrosia which drips
Onto thick wodges of bread.
The broad-leaved docks under the hives
Are like tongues expecting communion;
Interspersed among them are fingers of saffron
And violet sea lavenders. They point
To the weathered conifer tree
Behind the middle hive. Stumps indicate
Careful lopping of lower branches.
The upper branches: a complex of elbows;
Stretched arms and spiney claws; net the sky.
To the left of the fir tree there is a small
Apple tree abundant with tough apples.
To the right there are pale pink flowers
Big as the faces of babies and detailed
As vulvas, they grow crammed within a small
Wooden noose. And even though I have
So much of you in focus, I feel
Unbalanced by the immense emptiness
Behind you. I'm afraid to look up
Beyond the details of your borders.
To look out of the garden is to risk falling.

II

It feels like hours as I look and look
At the details of our lives, as I listen
To a voice in my mind tell me again
She was with Samuel in the Union Bar
Laughing and drinking and later
Getting into his car.

Here is a jumble of cracks. The trees
Breed darkness. Even the cornfields
Lose their usual luminosity.
Men and women thresh corn
As a man with a stick directs children
Through another field.

Here is a muddied spade
Near three pots of clay. One is empty,
One full of soil, the third bears two frail flowers.
A ledge defines the minister's garden
Beyond is the wilderness.

III

When I stand very close to the canvas
The women become dots, shoals of fish,
Lush dominions of water. When I move
Far away they become wives and slaves.

Four women amble in front of the painting.
One wears bright orange socks, suede shoes,
Floral skipants and that's odd
She has no bum. One woman is in black

Jersey top, pleated skirt, leggings and boots.
She absorbs light from everything.
The other two women natter
Hiding behind their stiff expressions "bored bloody bored."

The woman with orange feet skates
From painting to painting. Her button eyes
Brim with colour – "They're so big" she says.
The two women smile and nod but do not

Stop talking; which is how it was with you.
And when I learnt you were half Spanish
Half Jewish I prepared myself
For a crusade of cultural exchanges

The Islamic Moors in Spain,
The quiet assertion of Judaism in Manchester
Or of the Muslims who have acquired and made
Sweat shops of the Manchester mills.

I mentioned Ramazan and Pesach
But you stumbled over the words
Halah and Korsher and promptly
Dived headlong into gossip

Which is not what I had in mind
I hoped to find a place in the minister's garden.
We could have grown okra and coriander
Alongside the cabbages and carrots.

HASLAM PARK

Against the deep red of freshly cut meat
These trees knit a gauze of darkness.

A small dog bounds back and forth
On the other side of the pond.
Slowly he becomes a pale rectangle of light.

His owner sits on a bench and lights
A cigarette. The flame is no bigger than Venus
Which glimmers above him.

He looks, across the pond, at us
And sees two ebony statues
On a bench. He looks up
Above the wider arc of the trees
Where ducks freewheel
Like blackfish; circling a bowl
Of air, the base of which
Is this black pond.

A woman in a crimson raincoat
Scrapes her feet by the edge
Of the water. Bothered
By our presence, she walks
Back into the dark.

Two by two the ducks swoop down
Fold their wings and fall
The last six feet or so.

Beneath the slap of their bellies
Luminous ripples spread.
It's as if all the light
From the sky had drained into this pond
And just below the surface, within our grasp
Is a world of light.

Trwyn Cilan

There is nothing symmetrical here.
Not the askewed surfaces of the tides
Not the boulders, not the stones
Not even the spheres of sand.

A clump of seaweed rooted in the sea bed
Tumbles, jerks sideways, flops and then
Implodes, clenching tight the battered nodules
Only to splay open again, vulnerable
As always to those undercurrents.

A boy and a man, trample across the bay.
They ignore the sand pickled gull
And agree on a particular rock as a target.
The boy bowls the pebbles;
The man hurls the stones
Finding little comfort
In the metaphor he has found.

Hoof and paw-prints mish mash
Over and over as a black dog scampers
After the woman on horseback.
Light bounces off their faces.

Five oyster catchers sweep overhead.

A fat man drags in the nets.
The chequered frayed ropes have caught
Green and purple seaweed
Nothing else.

TREFOR

Sunlight is cut by the blunt edges
Of the slate gutted mountains.

Tidal waves break
Through coves, crooks and corners.

Spume shoots up and then
Drops, like white pebbles,

In the receding swell
Casting lots of soluble rings.

The frontiers of the sea
And the land shifts

With the crisscross of tides.
I visualize the moon, beneath

My feet, through the many miles
Of earth and space, effecting

These waves, tracing out
Time curves along the shore.

"Look, look a boat," shouts
My son of three. I barely

Make out the tiny white sail
Trembling on the thin edge.

J.B.

Something moves through us
Making the bone joints tingle a little.

Your hair has caught three flakes of ash
Which could be easy to pick
But before I can touch, you go off
In another arc
Down the slope
Into the dark
And back up again
To stop elsewhere.

Clickety clack comes from an acre of black
Tiny lit cabins rush across invisible tracks
A ball of light disappears in the black
Come back, come back, come back.

We were surprised when the guide said
Lancaster town was once known as the hanging town
Families would travel for miles
Just to see a good day's hanging.

Bored with dungeons and tools of torture
You left the castle before we learnt of the girl
Who became so weak they made her a wheel chair
Just for the short journey to the gallows.

You have wandered far enough
For me to become one inch tall
A black figure held in the rims
Of your orange lit glasses.
Behind us the beacon sheds and sheds
Richer shades of orange.

Ghosts appear briefly from our mouths
Soon we will lose each other.

SLEEPING WITH BELINDA

In my dream I tried
To kill a bumble bee
Flattening it with a book

But it burrowed through
So I struck it with a very thick
Paperback and was frightened

When it bored through that
So I slammed it between two
Hardbacks and that was that.

I chucked the four books
And the thin bee into the fire.
When I poked the ashes, up

Floated a golden bumble-bee and
It was angry – I was done for – staked
And wide awake to her loud snoring.

DAVID

Crouches before the inscribed slab.
His father's name. Words in Hebrew.
A soiled door shut on silence.
His greying hair has thinned. Eyes closed,
Lips ajar, he nods before a wall of air.
There are no answers here
Only loss. Slowly from between
His fingers and his mouth
Light dissolves, darkness increases.

ANNE'S BAPTISM

She wears a Nuclear Free Seas T-shirt
And offers her testimony of "God is Mega"
To a packed hall. And even before
She is waist deep, they bless her
In the name of the Father, the Son
And the Holy Ghost.

And it seems as if she is held underwater
For ages, fixed in that pure glassy bed
Like some Egyptian Queen; and even before
She is fully risen, she gasps for air
Like one just born as they receive her
With their hosannas and psalms
Meshing spirit with water and flesh.

And soaked through and through she mouths
To her mother I love you
And her mother who is robed in red
Becomes a big throbbing heart
As Anne pads out of the pool.

And in her absence from the hall
As she changes into dry clothes
Her presence lingers amongst us
As ripples bounce from the sides of the pool
As ripples criss-cross and begin to cancel
As arcs of light ascend the brown curtains.

And I will ask Wendy and Aleem if they believe
And she will reply no and he will say
Born and bred as a muslim I cannot help
But believe in something.
And Mark will say he wants to be a Mahayana Buddhist.

Brenda will hide her arthritic hands
In the sleeves of her overcoat
And she will amuse the boys
With her story of the Arabian masseur
Who tore off her swimsuit in one go.
Mark will half quote the Lord's Prayer in Latin;
And Tim shall down the night with even more pints;
And each of us will turn our backs
To the dark and go our separate ways.

But look here comes Anne
With so much light shining from her face
As she joins David and Diana
As now she lifts her slender hand
Waving in the air
An invisible beacon of strong undying light:

May its strength give her strength;
May she find inner peace and joy;
May she wake up in Zion.

A String of Knots

I've asked to stop again
To rest, to sit, to catch my breath
And breathe in the view
As seen from here.

You begin to talk geometrics
To reduce the landscape into several
Two dimensional planes.
The first is a third way
Down the valley, marked
By a tree which you describe
As an arc filled with an x number of triangles.

It could be an emerald Japanese fan
Behind which the beautiful Madame Butterfly hides.

The second plane contains the oval lake.
A big silver fish with shiny scales.

Consider the relationship
Between the waves and the air;
Those hard mobile surfaces are well defined
However on a molecular level there is a mist;
Molecules of water and air kiss and couple
As they make and break strong and weak forces.

The third and fourth planes
Contain the silhouette of mountains.

Your fingers part my hair
As an arrow of geese
Ascends through each of those flat planes.
The wind strikes the lake
As if each wave were piano keys;
The trees bend under the swift
Pressure of many violin bows.
Slowly the weakest force of all
Summons the flaky moon
And the faint promise of Venus.

She makes music with her fingers.
The snowman resonates in the timber
Of her house which becomes
The cool interior of her Baby Grand.

Upstairs he runs the bath.
Sunshine mixes with steam. He opens
His red mouth and fills the house
With extracts from Puccini's La Bohème.

In the kitchen light catches
The serrated edges of the bread knife.
He slices three generous portions of poetry
Tips the sun to his lips; drinks cappuccino.

MUD PEOPLE

Leaving Tesco with a boot full of food
We turn left into Broad Road.
Pebbles of light dance
Across the windscreen.

Listening to the radio
We coast past apple trees.
Apple blossoms yawn in the sun
As the voice across the air waves

Speaks of the Elite Guard
Who captured some Kurds
Tied their hands and feet
And threw them in the river.

Heads bobbed in the water – bullets
Broke bone – pink ribbons of light
Drift through pink blossoms.
Pink blooms in the car

And I see myself driving
In slow motion, my mouth open
The car slipping into the dark
Hush of the willow trees

And the news reader speaking
About Bangladesh. Houses of mud
Swept away in floods. The winding
Streets, the arteries bloated

With tidal waves of slush.
And after the cyclone
A shallow ocean of open graves.
Light glistens across the black

Water, dark limbs fester. Slowly
I turn left into Temple Road.

It seems as if the cat
Appeared from the slabs beneath our feet.
The strata colours of its fur are the same
As that of the mossy gravestones.

I try to ignore her as she rubs
Her back against my legs. You kneel
And stroke her head. She follows us
Into the church. You sit on a ledge

In the sun, perfect and unassuming.
I construct the absent roof and walls
Of the church with blue slates
And boulders of sunlight. We find

Stillness and tranquillity in ourselves.
Around us there is loud chatter
By blackbirds, thrushes, magpies and common birds
They leap through clear walls of light.

The cat accompanies us to Sylvia's grave.
It's an old Jewish tradition to bring a stone
For the dead; and an Islamic one
To bring some soil, as a mark of respect,

I tell you as I crumble some earth
And place a pebble on her grave.
No other words come to mind. There is only
The hurt of strong sunlight and the shock

Of all these weeds. Slowly we move
To the shadows of the trees.
The leaves sigh
Remember, remember us.

I

Everyone at Celia Clyne
Is on holiday for the Sukkoth.

Meanwhile Shah and Sons work
Round the clock knitting jumpers.

We take a breather after
Printing the millionth label.

Around the mill court yard Mr Yan
Walks his monstrous Rottweiler.

Steve sucks
A cigarette and comments

"Did you hear that he spoke
To his dog in Chinese!"

"Oh and what language should
He speak to his dog in – English?"

II

Luminous ripples of ash blue
Drift from the tv and lap
Around my legs. I dip my hands
In the apparition of the Ganges
That thunders through the Himalayas
In this documentary. I look up
And see between the detached houses
A dark sycamore tree, perfectly detailed
Against the water white sky.
I watch the faint silhouette
Of my parents, reflected in the window,
Fill up as the dark outside spreads
Generously. Now they are luminous,
Almost out of my reach, as now
They bow before Allah and I hear
Their salwars ruffle behind me.
In the kitchen
The fan hums as Uzma places cutlery
Around the table. Upstairs Khalid listens
To the Stone Roses. Qasim looks bleakly
At his future among his GCSE options.
Soon Lubna will be home from Hull University
And we shall say Bismillah-i-Rah-man-ir-Raheem
Over allo goshte and pilau rice.

HER HANDS

Patiently she points at her wrist
Again and again. Time.
She spells the word aloud in her mind.

He was so intelligent, she tells him
And only partially deaf
When some skins had clubbed him senseless.

She plucks light from the air
As she converses with a girl
Whose eyes light up.

He watches her hands
Move like the heads of swans
Become paper and pen
Touch mouth and heart
Fold up into a ball
And as she looks at him
She separates them far apart.

On Losing her Soul

She has finally come home
Bringing in her arms
The broken limbs of her soul
Crossing the musty hall
Neither as a bride nor as a widow.

She has finally come home
To give up her aching bones
To place the gossamer ruins
Among the broken spines of books
Among mountains and lovers
Stars and deserts, spices and people.

She has finally come home
To unload and confront all the wrong
To loosen and crush the charred heart
Of her soul; to let her hands and limbs
Dissolve in the dark, to kiss goodbye
The last splinters of light.

ON LOSING HIS SOUL

He wanted to stake his soul
To watch it writhe and struggle.

He wanted to dissect and determine
The quality of its light.

He purchased chloroform, acids
Sharp implements and linen; and

While he debased himself, he felt
His soul flee through the pores

Of his skin, leaving him in a cold sweat.
Now he wakes at odd hours in the night

And he eats raw fish to fill the emptiness
He feels. His head breeds darkness.

Demons of a richer darkness gather
Around him: and he goes out to eat the light

Of lost souls. On good nights, the dark
Within his eyes is so pure, it shines.

Ivy

I

In the summer you had grown wild
Butting through the gutters,
Roaming across glass and pronging
Into the blue air. Rogue.

We lopped you out of the drains
Away from the windows and
Trimmed you close to the brick.
When we propped the ladders

In the thick middle of you
A blackbird flashed out –
Its brief span of wings
Was braided with sunlight.

As I gouged you with the shears
Several domestic birds sprang out
And two furry moths tumbled in my face
Brushed my eyes and stumbled into space.

I gripped the ladders as my heart
Fluttered up my throat. Taking deep breaths
I steadied myself, then with weak wrists
I parted the blades, slowly.

II

From the frosty air I have plucked
This ivy branch which had grown
On the frame of my bedroom window.
On one of its tiny feet
There is a spot of white paint.
I fold and twist the twig in my hand
Clench it close to my face;
It smells of leaves burning.
My palm tingles with electricity
I feel our molecules mix
Exchange secrets and fears
The mysterious goings-on
Around this house. Strangers
Arriving and leaving. Movement
Of shadows in the moonlight. A sleek
Creature, white fangs, hooked claws.

Ivy you and I are strangers
Sleeping in the same house
But I feel I know you
Now that we are molecule brothers
Now that your veins
Grow in me and your leaves cling
Around the walls of my head.
Our secret underworlds
Overlap and I begin to wonder
How wild I have grown, what
Creatures harbour in me
And where have I left those shears?

ABAGEE'S THEKAN

Fat aubergines gleam
With a violet South African light
The kind seldom seen here in Rusholme.
It is a light laced with the scents
Of green and red chillies; plaited
With endless bushes of coriander;
Grained with the soil of Kenyan okra.

It has that frail luminous feel of Israeli air
Heaped among these near perfect suns. It is a light
Granulated into millions of milky Basmati grains;
Clumped solid into tough cloves of Spanish garlic.

No two shades of yellow, nourished by the same sun,
Grown on any branch of any tree are ever the same.
Mangoes from Bombay are fit to burst
With different stories of the same summer.
Saint Lucian bananas promise of hot
Secluded beaches and a cool coral sea.

Last night torrential rain has left
Contours of the Sahara desert
Across our window sills and cars.

FOR POPPY

Look it's there again, red light
Green light shining in the tree.
It's like magic, is it magic?
In the middle of that fir tree

Hangs a sack of light, a bag
Of water, an opaque trembling heart
Which pumps a rainbow of colours
Against the conifers in our garden.

I could tell you that the branches
Are heavy with dew and the wind
Has swung one such drop to cause light
To diffract in the spectral of red

And green, but your tender fingers
In my tired hands will not allow
Such explanations. Instead we say
It is the ear ring of the Snow Queen

Or the eye of a huge green goblin
Or tears from the prince who searches
For Snow White or Goldilocks.
It could be a beacon to guide

Lost souls out of thick invisible woods,
Or it is the gateway to another
World, full of such light. My love
It is the promise of paradise.

UNCLE JALIL

He crouches carefully to minimise
The pain from his fractured rib.

Sometimes we get hot sunny days
In winter and the trees think
Spring has begun; their juices flow
They make tender buds which get killed
A week later by the hard frost.
To prevent this deception I have painted
The trunks white so the heat is reflected.
One day I will put metal netting around
The trunks to stop rabbits eating them.

He supports himself with the trunk, rises
Slowly, uncurling the two scars which run
From the inside of his thighs to his ankles.

Oh Lord he sighs as the deep scar
Down his chest flexes. He explains
How they cut him open, twice
How they spliced blood vessels from his legs
To his tired heart and gave it a massage.
Now he grows these trees as therapy –
Something to look forward to each season.

This apple tree for example will produce
Pink, red and white blossoms; British pipin;
American grepner and Turkish tasha apples.
And this plum tree has American red hearts
Growing alongside Japanese yellow plums.

For a successful graft
You need to make a clean cut
On a branch of the tree and
The desired branch, twine the two firmly.
To speed up the healing
Tie strips of black bin bags around the join
This will give it extra heat.

In spring when they are in full blossom
It's wonderful, all those colours and scents
From all those countries, in my garden. Ahmen.

LAKE CARLTON

It isn't the water that travels
Under the wind but the wave.
The water simply arcs and unravels
In itself again and again.

It isn't the light that surfs
On the crest of those waves
But the arch of the waves
Simply reflecting the light.

It isn't the dark ripples
That are flowing across the lake floor,
But the shadows of the forward
Travelling wave and nothing more.

Today insects will not settle on the lake
And so the fish will not break
The surface for an easy kill; which means
Kestrels, egrets and vultures will not be seen.

I almost told my mum about the baby turtle
That popped up its head to say hello
But the faint sound of my voice
Bouncing back from space between

Manchester and Mount Dora surprised me
As if my soul, weak and lost somewhere
Spoke back each word to me:
I miss you also… don't worry I'll be home soon.

P.R.

All my sinews are slack.
Carefully you work the soft of your palm
Across the upper vertebrae of my back.

Just by my last rib
You funnel your fingers to a point
And begin to shovel and dig.

Flesh opens to flesh opens to a lake
Gateway to my soul in which I feel
Your arm twist and slide like a snake.

I love your face. I love its calm
Openness. Can you hear the dolphins
Singing in my heart the love psalm?

I want so much to enter your garden
To eat your apples by the tree load and when
We are full, to read you poems by W.H. Auden.

But alas it has become plain
I'm just another client and your job
Is your job; we will not pass this way again.

You have moved on to squeeze
The ridges of my legs. Funny how I
Can't stop, within myself, the big freeze.

You ask me to listen to the sounds
In the hall, hook my mind to them
And come back slowly to the ground.

Only I don't, I won't.
I open my eyes and sit up
Far too soon. Strange but I want

To smoke and chat
But my voice has gone too deep
So I walk away and do not look back.

I've counted fourteen different
Patterns of ceramic tiling
On the same floor! As I sketch
The red almond shapes
Among grey and fawn rhomboids
A Cypriot hums and hops
Over broken columns and boulders.

For all I know his history
Might go back as far
As these roman ruins.
My history can be traced beyond the Moguls.
Here we are, two strangers from distant empires
On common ground; unable to speak
A common language so we just nod.

I suppose there was a time
When the sun must have set
Along the doorway of this magnificent house;
And the lady of the house
Surrounded by slaves, who fed her
Oranges and figs, must have seen
The sun, go down as it does now
Into the Troodos mountains.

In this halflight
I feel our easy breathing mix
As the black silhouettes of modern blocks
Mingle with the houses and medina of the ancient town.

I don't know why, when the sun has gone,
Sections of the sea become opaque, almost shine.
It's as if light lost among the depths
Is given back to the sky from such gateways
As a shining sword or a huge scimitar
Or a spread of wings.

Bats volley in the dark.
Their clumsy flight is much the same
As when the lady turned
To go back inside, as when
The imam called everyone to prayer
As we politely wave
And go our separate ways.

My father is deep among
Circuit diagrams, looking
For familiar symbols.
"Diodes will allow current
To flow in one direction
Only; like some passages
Crammed with pilgrims in Mecca."

He locates the connections
Of the switch from the map
To the electronics. Test wires
Loop between my fingers like
Veins. I follow instructions
And make the link between two
Points; "This part of the circuit

Is fine." "Try the one marked six."
"That's it, this one is faulty."
I unscrew the switch, hand it
To my father who whispers
A short prayer, then opens it.
After much thought he decides
To turn a plastic grub clock-

Wise by ninety degrees. I
Reassemble it and make
The relevant connections.
My father says Bismillah
As I plug the machine in
And the main fuse does not blow;
So far so good. We have faith

In electronic diagrams
Symbols and components and
Something beyond. I have some
Knowledge of electronics but
None of the Koran and its
Beautiful verse; the letters
Are symbols; complex diagrams

Of the soul. My father can
Read a little of both. Just
Then the machine fails and we
Go back to the diagrams
Running short of ideas and
Hope, but with our faiths open
Unshaken and connected.

PAINT BOX

Stripped of carpets and wallpaper
My house has become a space for echoes.
I'm somewhere in my past
Up a ladder with gloss white in my hands
And now in the front room
Wiping Sahara matt from the wood.

The phone rings and rings
I hear it ringing
Long after I have said hello;
My words, my pauses, my breath
Are charged by the second.

I breathe paint into my head
I give, some of the paint
Back to the air, some
To cover imaginary walls
And the rest goes elsewhere.

I watch my fingers lose grip
(Again) of that can of paint
Which takes a life time to fall
And now, younger still,
I'm applying salmon pink
To the skirting of our old house;
I hear the radio
(Amplified on the wooden floor),
The fat voice of the famous song writer
"I ran away from home
When I was very young,
And I joined a touring band
And I never looked back."

It's funny, after all the travelling,
To find myself here, back home.
My friend tells me how he ran
Fast, then slow, then fast
Through the City
And now he's so exhausted
He wishes he hadn't.

We arrange to meet soon.
Time and space converge
Around the nib as I scribble
In my diary London, Linden
On the dates which become the past.

The last chime of the bell subsides
Before we have said our goodbyes.
I follow my footsteps up
The wooden stairs. Soon
The carpet will be put down
The bedroom and study fitted
And my friends will come round
With gifts and bottles of wine
Already I can see their souls
Moving through the yellow
Lilac and orange rooms. The air
Accommodates for all
Our warmth and echoes.

THERE IS NO NEED TO LOOK

Behind this wall where my parents
Read the Zuhr Namaz
Create small whirlpools of air
As they bow, pause then kneel.

The solid silence of Allah is uninterrupted
By the ruffle of selwar chemise
By the rasp of knife slicing lettuce
By the ripping of sheets and polystyrene.

There is so much light in the kitchen
I barely make out Khalid's outline;
And even though I am half way
Up the stairs, I still see him
Through the floorboards and plaster
A figure of light dabbing skinned potatoes
With Olive Gold. I taste the warm
Breath of my mum and dad
As I enter Uzma's bedroom; where Qasim
Plays Imagine on his new Yamaha keyboard.
I open a book on Tai Chi. Outside I know
The leaves are turning brown. I know
The sky is packed with sunlight
And the dark bony crosses are really
Seagulls. There is no need to look.

MAKING SHADOWS

All we need is chalk, some water
And a sponge just in case. We don't
Mind being up so early to remember
The lost fathers, mothers, sons and daughters.

When I lie down on paving stones or concrete
For you to trace my outline, I won't
Vaporize into thin air nor be dismembered
Nor burn nor choke to death; I
Will be able to lift myself to my feet
And walk away, I can always walk away.

We are careful not to be seen
As I lie down by the wool shop
In Uppermill and as you lean
Over me with chalk in hand, you stop
For a moment and look into my eyes
And I notice the blue of your iris
Happens to match with the morning sky.
We smile, then in silence
You bring the chalk down in slow
Motion and it looks as ominous as the point
On the big Fat Boy and as you go
Around my shoulder, arm, warm joint
Of wrist, the grind of chalk on stone
Sounds like the gasps of many
Breathing their last as every bone
In every person vaporised with nothing
To show of their lives but the white outline
Of their souls; crossing roads or waiting
By bus stops or making a call, just
The usual everyday things. Today it's a fine
Sunny morning. You wring chalk dust
From you hands and then we look
For a long time at the drawn figure
By our feet, empty just empty. Many books
Have detailed accounts of that day
But of today, I would like to say
How glad I am to run my fingers
Through your hair, to touch your crown
And kiss your lips and linger
As long as I like in your arms.

55

Tell Her

that one poem follows another
that two seeds yield a forest
that ice, water and steam are the same
that none of the four elements are elements
that our fifth finger evolved into a thumb
that breath connects us to all life
that each breath makes up a moment
that each moment is different
that I have learnt to forgive myself
that there are more than ten ways of saying
I love you
that light is infinite and finite
that I am here and elsewhere
that nothing escapes dark matter
that I do what I can for us and them
that satellites bring the world
into the corner of our living room
that we are ugly and beautiful
that the older I get the more
I am drawn to silence.